Jo Told My Therapist

Plus cartoons, tall tales, and funny true stories

If you have ever been offended, please do not read this book.

Written and illustrated by

Philip Copitch, Ph.D.

Copyright © 2012, Philip Copitch, Ph.D., Incorporated

All rights reserved. No part of this book may be reproduced or transmitted in any form or by any means, electronic or mechanical, including photocopying, recording, or by any information storage and retrieval system, without written permission from the author.

In other words: Please pay for your copy so that we can keep producing valuable information.

Written and illustrated by Philip Copitch, Ph.D.
Printed in the United States of America.

HERE TO SERVE YOU:

Hutzpah Press titles are available in quantity discounts for promotions, premiums and fundraisers.

FOR FURTHER INFORMATION PLEASE CONTACT:

HUTZPAH PRESS
PO BOX 400
IGO CA 96047-0400

Geri Copitch, Sr. Editor
Geri@CopitchInc.com

Dr. Phil's website:
www.CopitchInc.com

Dr.Phil's website: www.CopitchInc.com
or funnies at: http://peopletoons.blogspot.com
T-shirts / mugs: http://www.zazzle.com/copitch*

Dedication

Thanks Geri, the love of my life!

I do appreciate that you put up with my sense of humor.

Special thanks to:

Geri Copitch
Ken Hanson
Phyllis Bobrow

And:
Research - Sara Bellum, Will Power, Ben Dover
Catering - Al K. Seltzer, Al Dente, Chris P. Bacon,
  Sam Manilla, Luke Warm
Design - Art Major, Page Turner
Costumes - Beau Tye
Medic - Emma Royds
Security - Ray Gunn, Pat Downe
Insurance - Pearl E. Gates
Driver - Rick Shaw, Joy Rider
Animal wrangler - Sal A. Mander

Tell me, I forget.
Show me, I remember.
Involve me, I understand.

Table of Contents

Introduction	6
I have a few rules about jokes	8
1. Jokes to tell to kids (Rated G)	9
2. Back talk jokes great for teens (PG13)	45
3. Jokes you should never tell children	95
4. Tall tales	222
5. True stories	235
Hippie therapist	235
Satan and the chickens	236
The drunk at 7–11	238
Uncle Joe's Eye	238
My mom had one joke	240
My mom and the two liter bottle of coke	240
My mom and the ambulance driver	241
When Garry and I visited mom after being away for a long time.	242
Sleeping on the hide-a-bed	244
Mom and the new TV	245
Geri Copitch and the San Francisco Airport	246
Michael and the teacher's dress	247
Michael skeeching down Monroe Avenue	248
Garry and the summer of holy cow	249
Expensive chocolate	250
Jazz and the obstacle course	251
Jazz goes to second grade	252
You're not fat, Dr. Phil…	253
Play nice	255
The poker game	256
Flat broke in Reno	257
Fun with words	258
The royal wedding	259

Gust's brother	260
Saturn and the girlfriend's new bird	261
Tommy the tortoise	262
Mountain Man	263
The bug man in the lady's bedroom	265
The bug man on the back porch	266
Out of the mouth of babes	266
Me and golf	267
When my mom first met my fiancée	267
Did God live in 5C?	268
Dr. Phil I thought you were gay	270
Friday Night Live	271
Ducks in the bathtub and goldfish in the toilet	272
Very depressed	273

6. Jokes my wife forbade me from telling again 275

7. In closing, my favorite jokes 285

8. Encore Cartoons 296

Introduction

I have been a therapist for over thirty years. It doesn't seem that long, except when I look in the mirror and think to myself, "There's an old fat therapist looking at me."

I have been fortunate to have worked with, and learned from, my patients. Often, when I am working with a depressed person, I give a simple homework assignment, "Bring me a joke you like to start the next session." So, I've heard a lot of jokes over the years.

Sometimes I use jokes to help me gauge how a patient is coping. For example, during a heated divorce I tend to use this one with angry men, "What do a hurricane, flood, and a wife have in common? ... At some point one is going to get your house!" When a divorced man can laugh at that joke, he is well on the way to restarting his life.

Humor is very healing. Enjoy!

1. ☆ ☆ ☆ ☆ ☆ ☆ ☆ ☆ ☆ ☆

Above each joke in this book you will find ten stars. If you want, you can rate the jokes. Every joke is numbered for easy reference. Every now and again I will give a few hints on how to tell a particular joke.

This reminds me of a joke:

2. ☆ ☆ ☆ ☆ ☆ ☆ ☆ ☆ ☆ ☆

Mark Numskull got arrested for stealing a slice of pizza. Since the crime occurred in California, and it was his third strike, Mark got life. (This isn't the joke, this part is true.[1])

New to the cell block, Mark kept his nose clean and cautiously watched everything. That first night after lights out, Mark asked his no-necked, muscle-bound, tattooed toting cellmate, "Rocky, I don't get what all the laughing was about today. Someone yelled out a number and everyone busted a gut laughing."

"Oh, that's the way we keep the peace," Rocky explained. "We lifers tend to have a short fuse and there used to be lots of fights over how to tell any particular joke. So we decided to memorize and number them all. When someone yells out a number, we tell the joke to ourselves and have a good laugh. This way no one has to die."

Over the next few weeks, Mark paid close attention to the jokes. He knew he had to learn to fit in. Then one lunch he bucked up the nerve to stand on a table and shout out a joke.

"14," he yelled.

Nothing. The cafeteria got really quiet and all the hardened inmates just stared at him.

He got really nervous and yelled, "37."

The silence was deafening. Mark sat down quickly and kind of hid behind Rocky.

That night after lights out, Mark asked Rocky what went wrong.

"Well kid," Rocky said in his best Yiddish accent. "Some people can tell a joke, and some can't."

---

[1] TORRANCE - A man who stole a piece of pizza last summer has been sentenced to 25 years to life in prison, sparking renewed debate over the state's tough "three strikes" sentencing law.

Jerry Dewayne Williams, 27, of Los Angeles was convicted of felony petty theft in January for taking a slice of pepperoni pizza from a group of children, ages 7 to 14, eating at Adam's Pizza on the Redondo Beach pier.
-EXAMINER NEWS SERVICES March 3, 1995.

"Uh ... Tell me about your motherboard?"

I have a few rules about jokes

- I never interrupt the joke teller no matter how often I have heard the joke or how poorly they are telling it. Let the joke teller have their moment. They are trying to add a little humor to your day.
- I think it is criminal for a listener to step on the joke teller's punch line. Let them enjoy telling the joke, don't be a party pooper.
- I refrain from ethnic and racist slurs when telling jokes. When telling a joke with ethnic people in it, it shouldn't be the ethnicity that is funny, it should be the situation.

1. Jokes to tell to kids (Rated G)

"Hi Frank."

My intent with this section is to offer jokes adults can tell to children. I hope you enjoy watching them laugh. When telling jokes to kids it is best to oversell the punch line. Large gestures and big smiles let kids get into the moment.

3.   ☆ ☆ ☆ ☆ ☆ ☆ ☆ ☆ ☆ ☆

Where do you get tough chickens from?
Hard boiled eggs!

4.   ☆ ☆ ☆ ☆ ☆ ☆ ☆ ☆ ☆ ☆

What do you get from an elephant's nose?
Two ten foot boogers!

I have told this joke to thousands of kids over the years. Once when I was in Costco a little kid pointed at me excitedly and yelled, "That doctor has ten foot boogers!" The mom was horrified. I was impressed that my little friend remembered me.

5.   ☆ ☆ ☆ ☆ ☆ ☆ ☆ ☆ ☆ ☆

How do you know if there has been an elephant in your refrigerator?
There are footprints in the butter.

6.   ☆ ☆ ☆ ☆ ☆ ☆ ☆ ☆ ☆ ☆

Why do elephants wear red tennis shoes?
So they can hide in cherry trees.

This must be a good camouflage for an elephant because I have never seen an elephant in a cherry tree. Have you?

7.   ☆ ☆ ☆ ☆ ☆ ☆ ☆ ☆ ☆ ☆

How do you catch a unique bunny rabbit?
You neek up on it.

8.   ☆ ☆ ☆ ☆ ☆ ☆ ☆ ☆ ☆ ☆

How come the animals on the ark didn't play cards?
Because Noah was sitting on the deck.

9. ☆ ☆ ☆ ☆ ☆ ☆ ☆ ☆ ☆ ☆

Why didn't the animals on Noah's ark play poker?
Why bother, they weren't allowed to have more than two of a kind.

Written by Geri Copitch

10. ☆ ☆ ☆ ☆ ☆ ☆ ☆ ☆ ☆ ☆

What do you call a frog that hops across the road, jumps into a mud puddle, and then hops back across that same road?
A dirty double crosser.

11. ☆ ☆ ☆ ☆ ☆ ☆ ☆ ☆ ☆ ☆

Have you ever been caught picking your nose in the closet?
Good hiding place isn't it?

12. ☆ ☆ ☆ ☆ ☆ ☆ ☆ ☆ ☆ ☆

Why do apes have such big nostrils?

(Wave your fingers in front of your nose)
Have you seen how big their fingers are?

13. ☆ ☆ ☆ ☆ ☆ ☆ ☆ ☆ ☆

You can tell longer jokes to kids, but you have to keep the story moving. It's important to keep an active picture flowing through the joke. Exaggeration is essential.

The last time I was in Los Angeles, I was amazed at how big the highways were. I was driving a rental car and just for fun, I got one of those convertible ones, you know the kind with no roof. It was just me and the sun. It was a beautiful day and I just loved the wind flying through my hair. As I was driving around, I found a truck driver who was standing by his giant refrigeration truck, the kind they use to carry ice cream to the stores. He was waving his arms and jumping around trying to get my attention. I pulled over to see what all the excitement was about.

"Hey mister," he said. "I really need your help."

"Sure, you need a ride?" I asked.

"Nah," he said. "My truck is broken and I need to get 20 penguins to the Zoo. Without the truck working I can't keep the penguins cool enough. Do you mind taking them to the zoo?"

"I'd be happy to. Let's get them into my convertible," I said.

So there I was with a bunch of penguins, a few snuggled together in each seatbelt, driving off to the zoo. I think they really liked the wind in their feathers. They liked to lift their little wings and pretend to fly as we sped off to the zoo.

Later that day, the penguins and I were walking down the street. The penguins were really friendly. I was the leader, and they waddled along behind me in a straight line.

Then I heard this giant truck horn and the truck driver I met in the morning yelled down from his truck window.

"Hey mister, I thought I told you to take those penguins to the zoo?"

"I did," I called back. "We had so much fun I'm now taking them for some ice cream."

14. ☆ ☆ ☆ ☆ ☆ ☆ ☆ ☆ ☆

Why does a gorilla always grab little kids by the ear?
Because he's trying to peel them!

15. ☆ ☆ ☆ ☆ ☆ ☆ ☆ ☆ ☆

What is the most expensive type of fish in the whole wide world?
A goldfish.

16. ☆ ☆ ☆ ☆ ☆ ☆ ☆ ☆ ☆

"Waiter, waiter, there's a fly in my soup!"
"Quiet," the waiter whispered. "Everyone will want one."

17. ☆ ☆ ☆ ☆ ☆ ☆ ☆ ☆ ☆

"Waiter, waiter, there's a fly in my soup!"
"What's it doing?" the waiter asked.
"The backstroke I think. No, I think it's attempting the butterfly."

18. ☆ ☆ ☆ ☆ ☆ ☆ ☆ ☆ ☆

"Waiter, waiter, there's a fly in my soup!"
"That could be, our cook used to be a tailor."

19. ☆ ☆ ☆ ☆ ☆ ☆ ☆ ☆ ☆

After a long day of skiing, a duck is in his hotel room and calls down to room service to have them send some lip balm up to his room.

A few minutes later, the bellhop is at the door with the lip balm.

"How would you like to pay for this, Mr. Duck?" the bellhop asks.

"Just put it on my bill."

"I see the problem. The cartoonist forgot to draw you a pair of nostril holes."

20. ☆ ☆ ☆ ☆ ☆ ☆ ☆ ☆ ☆ ☆

Who was the first person to have a computer?
According to the Bible, Eve had the first Apple.

21. ☆ ☆ ☆ ☆ ☆ ☆ ☆ ☆ ☆ ☆

Doctor: Nurse, how is that little girl doing who swallowed ten quarters last night?
Nurse: No change yet.

22. ☆ ☆ ☆ ☆ ☆ ☆ ☆ ☆ ☆ ☆

Why do kids have to go to bed?
Because the bed won't come to them!

23. ☆ ☆ ☆ ☆ ☆ ☆ ☆ ☆ ☆

What do you call a dog with no legs?
Why bother, he ain't coming!

24. ☆ ☆ ☆ ☆ ☆ ☆ ☆ ☆ ☆

"My dog is so smart, he knows lots of words," Bobby told his friends.

"No he isn't… he's just a dog," one friend said.

"No really," Bobby said. "He is really smart, watch!"

"Bounder, what's on the top of a house?"

"Roof."

"What's the stuff around trees called?"

"Bark, bark."

"What do you say if you see an owl carry off a cow?

"How owl?"

"What do you say if you see a really pretty girl poodle?"

"Bow,Wow, Wooow!"

"Now Bounder, this one is really hard," Bobby told his dog. "What does sandpaper feel like?"

"Ruff, Ruff!"

25. ☆ ☆ ☆ ☆ ☆ ☆ ☆ ☆ ☆

Why did the chicken cross the playground?
To get to the other slide.

26. ☆ ☆ ☆ ☆ ☆ ☆ ☆ ☆ ☆

Bobby was bragging about his dog Bounder again.

"Last night Bounder ate a firefly then he barked for hours with de-light."

27. ☆ ☆ ☆ ☆ ☆ ☆ ☆ ☆ ☆

Knock-Knock!
Who's there?
Cargo!

Cargo who?
Car go *beep beep*!

28. ☆ ☆ ☆ ☆ ☆ ☆ ☆ ☆ ☆ ☆

How do you make a mail carrier very nervous?
Your mom gives you a new pet for your birthday that is half elephant and half dog.

29. ☆ ☆ ☆ ☆ ☆ ☆ ☆ ☆ ☆ ☆

What is black and white and red all over?
A penguin with a sunburn.

30. ☆ ☆ ☆ ☆ ☆ ☆ ☆ ☆ ☆ ☆

What is black and white and red all over?
A nun with a nose bleed.

31. ☆ ☆ ☆ ☆ ☆ ☆ ☆ ☆ ☆ ☆

What is black and white and red all over, black and white and red all over, black and white and red all over?
The nun with a nose bleed rolling down a hill.

32. ☆ ☆ ☆ ☆ ☆ ☆ ☆ ☆ ☆ ☆

What is black and white and read all over?
A newspaper. (If you don't know what a newspaper is, ask your grandparents.)

33. ☆ ☆ ☆ ☆ ☆ ☆ ☆ ☆ ☆ ☆

What is black and white, black and white, black and white, black and white, black and white?
A zebra caught in a revolving door.

34. ☆ ☆ ☆ ☆ ☆ ☆ ☆ ☆ ☆ ☆

Why did the squirrel cross the road?
To show his girlfriend he had guts.

35. ☆ ☆ ☆ ☆ ☆ ☆ ☆ ☆ ☆ ☆

Did you hear about the cook that got arrested for beating a dozen eggs?

36. ☆ ☆ ☆ ☆ ☆ ☆ ☆ ☆ ☆ ☆

What did the pig say when the butcher grabbed him by his cute little curly tail?
That's the end of me!

37. ☆ ☆ ☆ ☆ ☆ ☆ ☆ ☆ ☆ ☆

What did the daddy dog say to his three daughters when they were playing dress-up with their mommy's high heels?
"Hush puppies!"

38. ☆ ☆ ☆ ☆ ☆ ☆ ☆ ☆ ☆ ☆

What's big and green and sleeps at the bottom of the ocean?
Moby Pickle!

39. ☆ ☆ ☆ ☆ ☆ ☆ ☆ ☆ ☆ ☆

What's black and white and red all over?
A penguin with a really bad diaper rash!

40. ☆ ☆ ☆ ☆ ☆ ☆ ☆ ☆ ☆ ☆

What did the mayonnaise say to the refrigerator?
Close the door, I'm dressing!

41. ☆ ☆ ☆ ☆ ☆ ☆ ☆ ☆ ☆

"Doctor, doctor, can you help me out?"
"Sure," said the doctor. "Which way did you come in?"

42. ☆ ☆ ☆ ☆ ☆ ☆ ☆ ☆ ☆

This guy walked into a psychiatrist's office and said, "Doctor, I think I'm invisible."

The psychiatrist looked around and got freaked, "Who said that?"

43. ☆ ☆ ☆ ☆ ☆ ☆ ☆ ☆ ☆

This guy walked into a psychiatrist's office and said, "I believe I'm a pair of curtains."

"That's OK," said the psychiatrist. "Just pull yourself together."

44. ☆ ☆ ☆ ☆ ☆ ☆ ☆ ☆ ☆

"Doctor, how do I cure myself of sleep walking?"
"Sprinkle thumbtacks all over your bedroom floor."

45. ☆ ☆ ☆ ☆ ☆ ☆ ☆ ☆ ☆

This little boy went to see his doctor.
"Doctor, I think I'm turning into a frog," he said.
"So what's the big deal?" asked the doctor.
"I'm afraid… I don't want to croak!"

46. ☆ ☆ ☆ ☆ ☆ ☆ ☆ ☆ ☆

This guy walked into a psychiatrist's office and said, "Doctor, I feel like a dog."

"That's OK," said the psychiatrist. "Why don't you take a seat on the couch so we can talk?"

"But, I'm not allowed on the couch."

47. ☆ ☆ ☆ ☆ ☆ ☆ ☆ ☆ ☆

Teacher: Where is your homework?
Student: I lost it fighting this kid who said you weren't the best teacher in this school!

48. ☆ ☆ ☆ ☆ ☆ ☆ ☆ ☆ ☆

Teacher: How much is half of 8?
Student: Up and down or across?
Teacher: What do you mean?
Student: Well, up and down makes a 3 or across the middle leaves two zeros!

49. ☆ ☆ ☆ ☆ ☆ ☆ ☆ ☆ ☆ ☆

Teacher: Who invented fractions?
Student: Henry the 1/8th?

50. ☆ ☆ ☆ ☆ ☆ ☆ ☆ ☆ ☆ ☆

Teacher: Did Native Americans hunt bear?
Student: Only in the summer, it was too cold in the winter.

51. ☆ ☆ ☆ ☆ ☆ ☆ ☆ ☆ ☆ ☆

Why is Alabama the smartest state?
Because it has 4 A's and one B!

"Hubble, Hubble, Hubble..."

52. ☆ ☆ ☆ ☆ ☆ ☆ ☆ ☆ ☆ ☆

A lady from the YMCA came to my house collecting for the new swimming pool.

My dad said, "I'd be happy to help." Then he gave her a glass of water.

53. ☆ ☆ ☆ ☆ ☆ ☆ ☆ ☆ ☆ ☆

Why was the Egyptian girl sad?
Because her daddy was a mummy!

54. ☆ ☆ ☆ ☆ ☆ ☆ ☆ ☆ ☆ ☆

What kind of lighting did Noah use for the ark?
Floodlights!

55. ☆ ☆ ☆ ☆ ☆ ☆ ☆ ☆ ☆ ☆

When planet Pluto was demoted from planet to giant space rock, the following joke was very common with the under 10 types:

Why did Mickey Mouse take a trip into outer space?
He wanted to find Pluto!

56. ☆ ☆ ☆ ☆ ☆ ☆ ☆ ☆ ☆

What do you give an elephant with diarrhea?
Tons of room!

57. ☆ ☆ ☆ ☆ ☆ ☆ ☆ ☆ ☆

Two little kids were bragging about their fathers.
"My dad is an astronaut and he is scheduled to go to the moon!" the first kid said.
"Well if my dad was an astronaut he would go to the sun!" said the second.
"You can't go to the sun, it's too hot," growled the first.
"See, that shows how dumb you are. My dad would go at night!"

58. ☆ ☆ ☆ ☆ ☆ ☆ ☆ ☆ ☆ ☆

Did you know that moon rocks taste better than earth rocks?
It's because they're a little meteor.

59. ☆ ☆ ☆ ☆ ☆ ☆ ☆ ☆ ☆

A German shepherd applied for the job of Head of Security for an international package delivery company.
During the job interview the boss seemed

impressed, "Your resume looks very good, Army special forces, military police training, advanced bomb squad tactical training, and four years with the Federal Drug Task Force… but, do you speak any foreign languages?"

"Meow?"

60. ☆ ☆ ☆ ☆ ☆ ☆ ☆ ☆ ☆ ☆

A slight little girl of seven came into my office with her mother. "I have a joke for you," she said with a big smile. "What were you doing under there?"

Confused I said, "Under where?"

"Underwear!" she howled with laughter. "You said underwear!"

"You got me," I said as I covered my face feigning embarrassment.

61. ☆ ☆ ☆ ☆ ☆ ☆ ☆ ☆ ☆ ☆

Did you hear about the spy who got locked in a dark jail cell with no way out? All he had was one match, a mirror, and a table.

Because of his special training he was able to get out.

He lit the match and looked in the mirror to see what he saw. He took the saw and cut the table in half. Two halves make a whole, so he crawled out.

62. ☆ ☆ ☆ ☆ ☆ ☆ ☆ ☆ ☆ ☆

The pony was having a hard time talking because he was a little horse.

63. ☆ ☆ ☆ ☆ ☆ ☆ ☆ ☆ ☆ ☆

What's invisible and smells like carrots?
Bunny rabbit farts.

64. ☆ ☆ ☆ ☆ ☆ ☆ ☆ ☆ ☆

Why does Piglet smell so yucky?
Because he always plays with Pooh.

65. ☆ ☆ ☆ ☆ ☆ ☆ ☆ ☆ ☆

Girl: Did you hear that Yogi Bear put band-aids all over his best friend?
Boy: How come?
Girl: Wouldn't you if you had a boo boo?

66. ☆ ☆ ☆ ☆ ☆ ☆ ☆ ☆ ☆

A doctor and a nurse were called to the scene of an accident.

Doctor: We need to get these people to a hospital now!
Nurse: What is it?

Doctor: It's a big building with a lot of doctors, but that's not important now!

67. ☆☆☆☆☆☆☆☆☆

"Mommy, can I go to the movies?" Ellen asked.
"I suppose, but how much is it?" Mom said.
"It will cost $27,569.54," Ellen said.
"What!" Mom said. "Why so much?"
"I want to go to the drive in," Ellen said, "but I don't own a car yet."

68. ☆☆☆☆☆☆☆☆☆

Bob phones for help.
"Fire Department, what is the nature of your emergency?"
"My house is on fire, come quickly!" Bob yells.
"How do we get to your house sir?"
"Umm, don't you still have those big red trucks?"

69. ☆☆☆☆☆☆☆☆☆

In a store, I was forced to hear two bickering siblings.
I got their attention and said, "Let's play the quiet game... you start."
It confused them long enough to bring peace to the cereal aisle.

70. ☆☆☆☆☆☆☆☆☆

What's the difference between broccoli and big green juicy boogers?
Kids won't eat broccoli.

71. ☆☆☆☆☆☆☆☆☆

What's green and hangs from trees?
Giraffe snot.

72. ☆ ☆ ☆ ☆ ☆ ☆ ☆ ☆ ☆ ☆

What did the hot dog yell when he crossed the finish line?
"I'm a wiener!"

73. ☆ ☆ ☆ ☆ ☆ ☆ ☆ ☆ ☆ ☆

The old man asked the bus driver, "Does this bus go downtown?"
"No sir," said the bus driver. "This bus goes *beep beep*."

74. ☆ ☆ ☆ ☆ ☆ ☆ ☆ ☆ ☆

Do you know why seagulls only fly over the sea?
Because if they flew over the bay, they would be bagels.

75. ☆ ☆ ☆ ☆ ☆ ☆ ☆ ☆ ☆

Did you hear? The cookie went to the doctor because he was feeling so crummy.

76. ☆ ☆ ☆ ☆ ☆ ☆ ☆ ☆ ☆

One lazy afternoon on the savanna, the ants challenged the elephants to a friendly game of soccer. Just before halftime, the game was tied 1 to 1, and the best striker for the ants got a breakaway. He was dashing unopposed down the right side of the field. The center fullback for the elephants was caught out of position. In a mad dash, he stampeded to the ball and "Wamp!" The elephant stomped on the ant——killing him instantly.

The whistle blew and the referee chimp ran over as he pulled out his red card. "What was that! You can't stomp on the opposing players!"

"I didn't mean to," the elephant cried, "I was just trying to trip him."

77. ☆ ☆ ☆ ☆ ☆ ☆ ☆ ☆ ☆

Mom: Why are you crying Becky?
Becky: Because my teacher yelled at me for something I didn't do.
Mom: You got into trouble for something you didn't do?
Becky: Yeah, my homework!

78. ☆ ☆ ☆ ☆ ☆ ☆ ☆ ☆ ☆

"Bob, What do you call a deer with no eyes?"
Bob thought for a bit, "No idea."

"Do you smell carrots?"

79. ☆ ☆ ☆ ☆ ☆ ☆ ☆ ☆ ☆ ☆

Teacher: Why are you crawling, Fernando?
Fernando: Because you told me not to walk into your classroom late anymore.

80. ☆ ☆ ☆ ☆ ☆ ☆ ☆ ☆ ☆ ☆

Everyone in town knows that you never ever go down by the old mill house because there is a mean troll that lives there now.

Little Geri didn't believe the stories so she went down to the old mill house to find out the truth.

As she walked around back, she was confronted by a little angry looking man with green eyes, long yellow fingernails, and bad breath befitting his pointy rotten brown and green teeth.

"What are you doing here little girl?" the troll growled.

"Nothing, just walking," Geri said trying not to show fear.

"You're not allowed to be here, I'll have to teach you a lesson.

Pick up a handful of pebbles or I'll bite your face!" yelled the terrible troll. "Now eat the handful of pebbles or I'll bite your face."

Not wanting to have her face bitten by a crazed troll, Geri choked down the pebbles.

"Now, see that muddy puddle? Drink a big drink of it, or I'll bite your face," grunted the troll.

Geri reluctantly drank from the muddy puddle.

"Now begone from this place or I'll forget my manners and bite your face!" screamed the horrible troll.

Geri ran and ran all the way home.

Later that day, Geri told her little brother that she went to the old mill house.

"Did you meet the troll?" Michael asked all wide eyed.

"Meet him," Geri bragged, "I had lunch with him."

81. ☆ ☆ ☆ ☆ ☆ ☆ ☆ ☆ ☆

What does a dog do that your dad steps in?
Pants.

82. ☆ ☆ ☆ ☆ ☆ ☆ ☆ ☆ ☆

Why do farts smell?
So deaf people can enjoy 'em.

83. ☆ ☆ ☆ ☆ ☆ ☆ ☆ ☆ ☆

A duck walks into a bar and flies up onto a stool. "Hey, barkeep got any grapes?"

The bartender is a little confused and says, "No."

The next day the same duck comes into the bar and asks, "Got any grapes?"

"No! Now get out of here!" growls the bartender.

The next day the same duck comes into the bar and asks, "Got any grapes?"

"I told you no, already... if you come in here again and bother me I'll nail your beak to this here bar," he says as he slams his hand down on the bar.

The next day the same duck comes into the bar and asks, "Got any nails?"

"No," said the confused bartender.

"Good! Got any grapes?"

84. ☆ ☆ ☆ ☆ ☆ ☆ ☆ ☆ ☆ ☆

What do you get if you eat too many beans and onions?
Tear gas.

85. ☆ ☆ ☆ ☆ ☆ ☆ ☆ ☆ ☆ ☆

"You have to eat a tightrope walker everyday," mommy cannibal told her son.

"But I don't like tightrope walkers… they're too stringy," said the little cannibal.

"I know honey," mommy cannibal said, "but I want you to eat a balanced diet."

86. ☆ ☆ ☆ ☆ ☆ ☆ ☆ ☆ ☆ ☆

What do you call a boomerang that doesn't come back?
A stick.

87. ☆ ☆ ☆ ☆ ☆ ☆ ☆ ☆ ☆ ☆

A horse was tied to a fence post when a small dog startled him. The horse bobbed his head, all wide eyed, and stomped his front hoof.

"Sorry I scared you," said the small dog.

The horse lowered his head and sniffed the dog then said, "Well I'll be a monkey's uncle, a talking dog."

88. ☆ ☆ ☆ ☆ ☆ ☆ ☆ ☆ ☆ ☆

Did you hear the story of the blind man who picked up a hammer and saw?

89. ☆ ☆ ☆ ☆ ☆ ☆ ☆ ☆ ☆ ☆

Do you know why Noah didn't fish much?

Because he only had two worms.

90. ☆ ☆ ☆ ☆ ☆ ☆ ☆ ☆ ☆

Where did the king keep his little armies?
Up his little sleevies.

91. ☆ ☆ ☆ ☆ ☆ ☆ ☆ ☆ ☆

What's brown and sticky?
A stick.

92. ☆ ☆ ☆ ☆ ☆ ☆ ☆ ☆ ☆

Something to think about:

Knowing that all your uncles are aunts must be very confusing for ant children.

93. ☆ ☆ ☆ ☆ ☆ ☆ ☆ ☆ ☆

Phyllis crept into her parents' room late one night and gently woke her daddy up.
"Phyllis are you OK, Honey?" her daddy said.
"Daddy can you sign your name in the dark?" she asked.
"I guess so," Daddy said.
"Good, please sign my report card."

94. ☆ ☆ ☆ ☆ ☆ ☆ ☆ ☆ ☆

"Did you hear that Dean found a one thousand dollar bill?" Dr. Phil asked.
"No?" said Elli.
"Well he did. It was stuck on the face of a very expensive duck."

95. ☆ ☆ ☆ ☆ ☆ ☆ ☆ ☆ ☆

Did you hear that Billy the buffalo was embarrassed as he was getting on the school bus? He was mortified when mommy buffalo waved and yelled from the porch, "bison!"

96. ☆ ☆ ☆ ☆ ☆ ☆ ☆ ☆ ☆ ☆

"Nurse I keep seeing yellow dots."
"Have you seen a doctor?" asked the nurse.
"No, just dots."

97. ☆ ☆ ☆ ☆ ☆ ☆ ☆ ☆ ☆ ☆

Mom said to dad, "I'm worried about our son. He named his new pet hamster, 'Goldfish'."

98. ☆ ☆ ☆ ☆ ☆ ☆ ☆ ☆ ☆ ☆

Corduroy pillows are making headlines!

99. ☆ ☆ ☆ ☆ ☆ ☆ ☆ ☆ ☆ ☆

What's the last thing to go through a bug's mind when he hits a windshield?
His butt.

100. ☆ ☆ ☆ ☆ ☆ ☆ ☆ ☆ ☆ ☆

Did you hear that all the toilet seats were stolen from the police station?
Really?
Yeah, the police have nothing to go on.

101. ☆ ☆ ☆ ☆ ☆ ☆ ☆ ☆ ☆ ☆

How do you get down from an elephant?
You don't. You get down from a goose.

102. ☆ ☆ ☆ ☆ ☆ ☆ ☆ ☆ ☆ ☆

Did you know that math books are the saddest of all books?
It's because they have so many problems.

103.   ☆ ☆ ☆ ☆ ☆ ☆ ☆ ☆ ☆

Did you hear that the silkworms had a race?
They ended in a tie.

104.   ☆ ☆ ☆ ☆ ☆ ☆ ☆ ☆ ☆

Why was the tomato red faced?
Because he saw the salad dressing.

105.   ☆ ☆ ☆ ☆ ☆ ☆ ☆ ☆ ☆

Humpty Dumpty had a great fall to make up for a truly lousy summer.

106.   ☆ ☆ ☆ ☆ ☆ ☆ ☆ ☆ ☆

Principal Thornbottom returned to his doctor looking all worn out and near death.

"Did you take the pills I gave you?" asked the doctor.

"Yeah, I sure did," said Principal Thornbottom weakly. "I did exactly what you told me to do... I took the pills for three days and then skipped a day."

107.   ☆ ☆ ☆ ☆ ☆ ☆ ☆ ☆ ☆

A snail got beat up by two hoodlum turtles. When questioned by the police the snail said, "I don't know, it all happened so fast."

108.   ☆ ☆ ☆ ☆ ☆ ☆ ☆ ☆ ☆

Little Bobby wanted a pet really badly. But his parents always said no! So he was sitting in the backyard under a tree crying when a centipede came walking up and said, "Why are you crying little boy?"

Bobby was amazed, and he told the centipede his troubles. After a while, the centipede suggested that he could be Bobby's pet. Bobby thought that was a great idea... a talking centipede as a pet!

Bobby made his centipede a lovely home with a house built out of Legos. He brought fresh grass and leaves for his pet everyday and they sat and talked together for hours upon end.

One morning Bobby asked his friend if it would be all right if he took him to school for show and tell. The centipede had never been to school and thought it was a great idea.

When it was time for the school bus to come, Bobby ran into his room with a jar with lots of air holes in its top. "Come on. It's time to go."

But the centipede didn't come out of his house.

"Come on, we're going to miss the bus," Bobby yelled.

Still the centipede didn't come out of his house.

Finally, in frustration, Bobby was banging on the house and yelling, "Come on, we're going to miss the bus!"

"Give me a minute," yelled out the centipede, "I'm putting on my shoes!"

109. ☆ ☆ ☆ ☆ ☆ ☆ ☆ ☆ ☆ ☆

"Waiter, waiter, there's a fly in my cereal!"
"That's not a fly, that's a raisin with wings."

110. ☆ ☆ ☆ ☆ ☆ ☆ ☆ ☆ ☆ ☆

"Waiter, waiter, will the pancakes be long?"
"No round."

111. ☆ ☆ ☆ ☆ ☆ ☆ ☆ ☆ ☆ ☆

"Waiter, waiter, there's no chicken in my chicken soup!"
"Of course not. There's no horse in the horseradish either."
"Very funny."
"I don't know what you mean, would you expect to find angels in angel cake?"

112. ☆ ☆ ☆ ☆ ☆ ☆ ☆ ☆ ☆ ☆

"Waiter, waiter, there's a fly in my soup!"
"I'm sorry sir. There is no excuse for that. I thought I got them all out."

113. ☆ ☆ ☆ ☆ ☆ ☆ ☆ ☆ ☆

"Dad, I'm going to a party, would you do my homework for me?"
"Of course not, it would be wrong."
"That's OK dad, as long as you tried."

114. ☆ ☆ ☆ ☆ ☆ ☆ ☆ ☆ ☆

Two sardines were startled when a huge submarine motored by.
"What was that?" said the first sardine.
"No need to worry," said the second sardine, "that's just a can of people."

115. ☆ ☆ ☆ ☆ ☆ ☆ ☆ ☆ ☆

What has four legs and one arm?
A very happy Rottweiler.

116. ☆ ☆ ☆ ☆ ☆ ☆ ☆ ☆ ☆

I was walking down the street and saw two guys trying to steal an old lady's purse. I've always believed in helping others with a problem, so I bit the old lady on the hand.

117. ☆ ☆ ☆ ☆ ☆ ☆ ☆ ☆ ☆

If you ever get cornered by a kid with a knock-knock joke book, (and who hasn't) use this joke.

Knock-knock.
Who's there?
Duey.
Duey who?
Duey have to keep telling knock-knock jokes?

118. ☆ ☆ ☆ ☆ ☆ ☆ ☆ ☆ ☆

"Waiter, waiter, this coffee tastes like mud!"
"That makes sense, it was ground this morning."

119. ☆ ☆ ☆ ☆ ☆ ☆ ☆ ☆ ☆

"Waiter, waiter, this food is not fit for a pig!"
"I'm sorry sir, let me get you some that is."

120. ☆ ☆ ☆ ☆ ☆ ☆ ☆ ☆ ☆

"Waiter, waiter, there's a dead fly in my soup."
"Makes sense… that soup is really, really hot."

121. ☆ ☆ ☆ ☆ ☆ ☆ ☆ ☆ ☆ ☆

Two high school kids went into a diner and ordered two sodas. Then they got sandwiches from their backpacks and started to eat. The waiter was upset and said, "You can't eat your own sandwiches in here!" The teens looked at each other, shrugged their shoulders, and exchanged sandwiches.

122. ☆ ☆ ☆ ☆ ☆ ☆ ☆ ☆ ☆ ☆

Did you hear about the new restaurant on the moon?
Great food but no atmosphere.

123. ☆ ☆ ☆ ☆ ☆ ☆ ☆ ☆ ☆ ☆

"Waiter, I'd like a cup of coffee please, with no cream."
"I'm sorry, sir, but we're out of cream. How about a cup of coffee with no milk?"

124. ☆ ☆ ☆ ☆ ☆ ☆ ☆ ☆ ☆ ☆

"Waiter, waiter, what is this stuff?"
"That's bean soup."
"I know what it's been, but what is it now?"

125. ☆ ☆ ☆ ☆ ☆ ☆ ☆ ☆ ☆ ☆

What do you call a man with a seagull on his head?
Cliff.

126. ☆ ☆ ☆ ☆ ☆ ☆ ☆ ☆ ☆ ☆

What do you call a man with a shovel stuck in his head?
Doug.

127. ☆ ☆ ☆ ☆ ☆ ☆ ☆ ☆ ☆ ☆

What do you call a man who is floating in the ocean?
Bob.

128. ☆ ☆ ☆ ☆ ☆ ☆ ☆ ☆ ☆

What has four wheels, one horn, and flies?
A garbage truck.

129. ☆ ☆ ☆ ☆ ☆ ☆ ☆ ☆ ☆

What time is it when an elephant sits on your alarm clock?
Time to get a new clock.

130. ☆ ☆ ☆ ☆ ☆ ☆ ☆ ☆ ☆

Why did your dad throw the alarm clock out the window?
He wanted to see time fly.

131.   ☆ ☆ ☆ ☆ ☆ ☆ ☆ ☆ ☆

In the dictionary there is always one misspelling.
The word *misspelling*.

132.   ☆ ☆ ☆ ☆ ☆ ☆ ☆ ☆ ☆

The longest word in the dictionary is smiles.
It has a *mile* between the s _ _ _ _ s.

"But Mom, I'm just making room for more presents!"

133.   ☆ ☆ ☆ ☆ ☆ ☆ ☆ ☆ ☆

"Can you spell the word Mississippi?" Smarty Smart Smart asked.

"Sure I can," said Joe.

"OK, spell it."

"M-I-S-S-I-S-S-I-P-P-I."
"Wrong!" said Smarty Smart Smart. "I asked you to spell *it*, I-T."

134. ☆ ☆ ☆ ☆ ☆ ☆ ☆ ☆ ☆ ☆

In school what is the best way to make straight "A's"?
Use a ruler.

135. ☆ ☆ ☆ ☆ ☆ ☆ ☆ ☆ ☆ ☆

Knock-knock.
Who's there?
Little Old Lady.
Little Old Lady Who?
I didn't know you could yodel!

136. ☆ ☆ ☆ ☆ ☆ ☆ ☆ ☆ ☆ ☆

Knock-knock!
Who's there?
Hatch.
Hatch who?
Bless you!

137. ☆ ☆ ☆ ☆ ☆ ☆ ☆ ☆ ☆ ☆

Knock-knock!
Who's there?
Ash.
Ash who?
Sounds like you have a bad cold.

138. ☆ ☆ ☆ ☆ ☆ ☆ ☆ ☆ ☆ ☆

What do porcupines say after they kiss?
"Ouch"!

139.

Where do you find a dog with no legs?
Right where you left him.

140.

"What are the four seasons?" the chef asked Mary.

"Spring, summer, fall, and winter," answered Mary.

"Nope... around here we season with salt, pepper, ketchup, and ranch."

141.

What kind of food is crazy about money?
A dough-nut!

142. ☆ ☆ ☆ ☆ ☆ ☆ ☆ ☆ ☆ ☆

Why is Cinderella so bad at sports?
Because she has a pumpkin for a coach, and she runs away from the ball.

143. ☆ ☆ ☆ ☆ ☆ ☆ ☆ ☆ ☆ ☆

Instead of getting angry, what did Cinderella say when her photos weren't ready?
"Someday my prints will come."

144. ☆ ☆ ☆ ☆ ☆ ☆ ☆ ☆ ☆ ☆

How do you catch a squirrel?
Climb a tree and act like a nut.

145. ☆ ☆ ☆ ☆ ☆ ☆ ☆ ☆ ☆ ☆

What's black and white and eats like a horse.
A zebra.

146. ☆ ☆ ☆ ☆ ☆ ☆ ☆ ☆ ☆ ☆

What did the carpenter say to the wall?
"One more crack out of you and I'll plaster you!"

147. ☆ ☆ ☆ ☆ ☆ ☆ ☆ ☆ ☆ ☆

What did the ground say to the earthquake?
"You crack me up!"

148. ☆ ☆ ☆ ☆ ☆ ☆ ☆ ☆ ☆ ☆

What did the duck say to the clown?
"You quack me up!"

149.   ☆ ☆ ☆ ☆ ☆ ☆ ☆ ☆

Who can shave six times a day, and still have a full beard?
A barber.

150.   ☆ ☆ ☆ ☆ ☆ ☆ ☆ ☆

Why is 6 afraid of 7?
Because 7, 8, 9.

151.   ☆ ☆ ☆ ☆ ☆ ☆ ☆ ☆

What's the difference between a guitar and a fish?
You can't tuna fish.

152. ☆ ☆ ☆ ☆ ☆ ☆ ☆ ☆ ☆

What did Ronald McDonald give Wendy for their engagement?
He got on one knee and gave her a golden brown onion ring!

153. ☆ ☆ ☆ ☆ ☆ ☆ ☆ ☆ ☆

"Grandpa, in school they taught me to sneeze into my elbow," Carlos said. "How come you just sneeze into your hand?"
"That way I can catch my teeth," grandpa said.

154. ☆ ☆ ☆ ☆ ☆ ☆ ☆ ☆ ☆

How do angels greet each other?
"Halo."

2. Back talk jokes great for teens (PG13)

When I was a kid, when TV was black and white, and kids would use one-upmanship to win power on the playground, the world was simpler. A little wit and fast talk ruled.

The worst thing you could do was to demean someone's mother, so... a lot of effort was put into attacking someone's mother with style.

155. ☆ ☆ ☆ ☆ ☆ ☆ ☆ ☆ ☆ ☆

Yo momma's so fat it takes two buses and a train to get on her good side.

156. ☆ ☆ ☆ ☆ ☆ ☆ ☆ ☆ ☆ ☆

Yo momma's so fat when she backs up her butt goes "beep...beep...beep".

157. ☆ ☆ ☆ ☆ ☆ ☆ ☆ ☆ ☆ ☆

Yo momma's so fat she had to get baptized at Sea World.

158. ☆ ☆ ☆ ☆ ☆ ☆ ☆ ☆ ☆ ☆

Yo momma's so fat when she walks across the room the iPod skips.

159. ☆ ☆ ☆ ☆ ☆ ☆ ☆ ☆ ☆ ☆

What did the elephant say to the naked man?
It's cute, but can you really breathe through that little thing?

160. ☆ ☆ ☆ ☆ ☆ ☆ ☆ ☆ ☆ ☆

How do you circumcise a whale?
Send down four skin divers.

161. ☆ ☆ ☆ ☆ ☆ ☆ ☆ ☆ ☆ ☆

Politicians and diapers should be changed regularly... for the exact same reason.

162. ☆ ☆ ☆ ☆ ☆ ☆ ☆ ☆ ☆ ☆

Yo momma's so fat she has her own zip code.

163. ☆ ☆ ☆ ☆ ☆ ☆ ☆ ☆ ☆ ☆

Scientist know that on the inside of a fire hydrant you'll find

H_2O and on the outside you'll find K_9P

164. ☆ ☆ ☆ ☆ ☆ ☆ ☆ ☆ ☆ ☆

Yo momma's so fat the national weather service tracks her farts.

165. ☆ ☆ ☆ ☆ ☆ ☆ ☆ ☆ ☆ ☆

Yo momma's so old she sat behind Jesus in the third grade.

166. ☆ ☆ ☆ ☆ ☆ ☆ ☆ ☆ ☆ ☆

Yo momma's so ugly that even in the third grade Jesus wouldn't play with her.

167. ☆ ☆ ☆ ☆ ☆ ☆ ☆ ☆ ☆ ☆

An Arkansas State Trooper spies a truck pulled off the road. The driver gets out of the cab with a tire iron and proceeds to walk along side his truck whacking each tire a few times.

Curious as to what's going on, the trooper follows the truck for a few miles until it pulls over and the driver again gets out and starts whacking the tires.

The trooper turns on his lights and pulls up behind the truck.

"What are you doing buddy?" the trooper asks the truck driver.

"Just following the law, officer," the truck driver says. "This here patch of highway is certified for 8 tons and I'm hauling 16 tons of parakeets. So every now and then I got to keep reminding half of them to keep flying."

168. ☆ ☆ ☆ ☆ ☆ ☆ ☆ ☆ ☆ ☆

A boy frog is told by a psychic, "You are going to meet a beautiful young girl who will want to know everything there is to know about you."

The frog is so excited, "This is great! Will I meet her at a party?"

"No," says the psychic, "in her biology class."

169. ☆ ☆ ☆ ☆ ☆ ☆ ☆ ☆ ☆

A lawyer was cross examining a doctor in a high stakes wrongful death case.

"So you're telling the jury that you did not check the vital signs of Mr. Thompson before you signed his death certificate?"

"That is correct, I did not," answered the doctor.

"Did you check to see if Mr. Thompson's heart was beating?" the lawyer said while he glared at the doctor.

"I did not," said the doctor.

"So it's your sworn testimony, in front of this court, that you did not examine Mr. Thompson's body to determine if he was dead?"

"Please let me explain," said the doctor. "His brain was in a jar on my desk, but for all I knew the rest of him could have been off practicing law somewhere."

170. ☆ ☆ ☆ ☆ ☆ ☆ ☆ ☆ ☆

The attorney was just coming out of anesthesia after major surgery.

"Am I alive?" asked the attorney. "Why is it so dark?"

"You're OK, Mr. Thornberg, There's a raging fire across the street so we closed the curtains. We didn't want you waking up and think you were… well, dead."

171. ☆ ☆ ☆ ☆ ☆ ☆ ☆ ☆ ☆

"Nurse, I'm shrinking," the scared man told the emergency room nurse.

"Hold on for a moment," she said. "You'll just have to be a little patient."

172. ☆ ☆ ☆ ☆ ☆ ☆ ☆ ☆ ☆

Anyone can have bad breath, but you could knock a buzzard off a manure wagon.

173. ☆ ☆ ☆ ☆ ☆ ☆ ☆ ☆ ☆ ☆

Yo momma's so short you can see her feet in her driver's license photo.

174. ☆ ☆ ☆ ☆ ☆ ☆ ☆ ☆ ☆ ☆

Yo momma's children are so ugly, that when they were born the doctor slapped yo momma!

175. ☆ ☆ ☆ ☆ ☆ ☆ ☆ ☆ ☆ ☆

Have you ever wondered why in the police locker rooms the lockers have locks on then? If police can't trust each other, how can we trust them?

176. ☆ ☆ ☆ ☆ ☆ ☆ ☆ ☆ ☆ ☆

Yo momma's children are so ugly, that when you were born, the nurse said, 'What a treasure' and your Daddy said, 'Let's bury him.'

177. ☆ ☆ ☆ ☆ ☆ ☆ ☆ ☆ ☆ ☆

An old farmer got himself all upset when he found a bunch of teenagers skinny dipping in his pond. He confronted them and told them the pond wasn't safe and they should get off his land.
One teen was feeling his oats and yelled from the water, "What you going to do old man, come in and make us get out?"
"Nope," yelled back the old farmer, "I don't want any trouble, I just came down here to feed the alligators."

178. ☆ ☆ ☆ ☆ ☆ ☆ ☆ ☆ ☆ ☆

One thing I can say about yo momma's cooking— it sure keeps the dog from begging at the table.

179. ☆ ☆ ☆ ☆ ☆ ☆ ☆ ☆ ☆ ☆

Yo momma's such a bad cook, the flies worked together to fix the screen door in the kitchen.

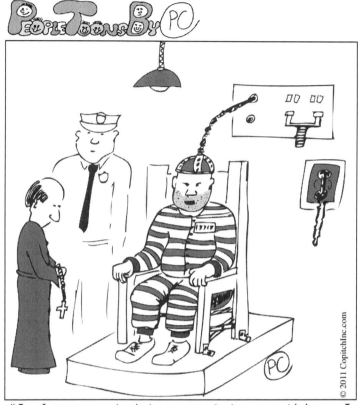

"I always wanted to amount to something. I guess I should have been more specific."

180.   ☆ ☆ ☆ ☆ ☆ ☆ ☆ ☆ ☆ ☆

How many flies does it take to screw in a light bulb?
Two. But I'm more curious about how they got in there.

181.   ☆ ☆ ☆ ☆ ☆ ☆ ☆ ☆ ☆ ☆

Mr. Morrison goes into the bar and finds a dog talking to the regulars. He pulls up a chair and listens as the dog tells stories about his time in the war.

"I worked for the CIA and I would be sent behind enemy lines. I'd act friendly to the enemy officers and they would feed me scraps.

In no time I would be able to hear all their war secrets. After a few days I would run back to my CIA handlers and tell them what I learned."

"One time I got close to a family. The kids loved me and their father was a high ranking general. For weeks I was able to read secret documents and at night I would radio back to base the secret information."

Mr. Morrison was amazed by this dog and he went to talk to the bartender.

"Do you know how valuable your dog is?"

"I'm not impressed," said the bartender, "because I know for a fact he didn't do half of that shit!"

182. ☆ ☆ ☆ ☆ ☆ ☆ ☆ ☆ ☆

A drill sergeant barked at his struggling recruit. "I bet when I die you're going to come to my grave just to pee on it!"

"Sir no sir," yelled the recruit. "When I get out of the army I'm not standing in any stinking lines again!"

183. ☆ ☆ ☆ ☆ ☆ ☆ ☆ ☆ ☆

Bob and Jake are out hiking and they come across a big hole. Out of curiosity Bob drops a rock down the hole, but they never hear it hit bottom. So Jake drops a bigger rock, again nothing. So they look around for something really big to drop into the hole. They find an old railroad tie and toss it in. Again nothing. All of a sudden a goat comes runny by and dives head first into the hole.

Bob and Jake are stunned when an old farmer comes out of the woods and says, "You boys seen my goat?"

"Yeah," said Jake. "One just dove into this hole."

"That can't be my goat— my goat was tied to a railroad tie."

184. ☆ ☆ ☆ ☆ ☆ ☆ ☆ ☆ ☆

"Momma," Sven said, "I have the biggest feet in the third grade, is that because I'm Norwegian?"

"No honey," momma said, "it's because you're sixteen."

"My blog wants to get this straight... for reals when you were a kid, Apple and Blackberry were just fruit?"

185. ☆ ☆ ☆ ☆ ☆ ☆ ☆ ☆ ☆

Billy Bob and Cletus are vacationing on the beach in Florida.

"The girls here aren't as friendly as they are back home," Cletus said.

"Why don't you put a potato in your swim trunks to impress the ladies," suggested Billy Bob.

A few hours later Cletus comes back to Billy Bob, "The potato isn't helping, the girls down here don't like me."

"Cletus," said Billy Bob, "you're suppose to put the potato in the front."

"I often have a dream where someone points at me and yells, 'BEAR!' This scares me 'cause I never know if it's me or if I'm naked."

186. ☆ ☆ ☆ ☆ ☆ ☆ ☆ ☆ ☆ ☆

After summer vacation in Florida, Cletus got a job painting highway lines back home. It was a good paying job but the boss was a real slave master.

On the first day, the boss told Cletus that it was expected that he paint two miles of highway every day.

At the end of the first day the boss checked Cletus' work and was happy to find that Cletus had actually painted four miles of highway lines.

On the second day, the boss checked on Cletus and found that he only did two miles of painting. On the third day the boss was not happy when Cletus only pained one mile of highway.

"Cletus my boy," the boss said, "I'm thinking of letting you go. You started out really good. How come you only painted one mile of highway in a whole day?

"Boss," Cletus said, 'I'm working as fast as I can, but the paint bucket is getting farther and farther away."

187. ☆ ☆ ☆ ☆ ☆ ☆ ☆ ☆ ☆

Mrs. Jacobson took her beloved Teacup Poodle, Coffee to the vet. The vet was very consoling, but the facts were that Coffee only had hours to live.

Mrs. Jacobson was beside herself with grief and demanded a second opinion. So the vet had his cat come in and examine Coffee. The cat shook her head sadly, agreeing with the vet's diagnosis.

Mrs. Jacobson was not convinced and demanded a third opinion. So the vet had Buster, his yellow lab, examine Coffee.

Buster sniffed Coffee and licked her gently. Then he lowered his head in sorrow and agreed with the vet's original diagnosis.

When Mrs. Jacobson got the bill she was outraged, "Nine hundred and eighty-three dollars to tell me that my beloved Coffee was dying! How come so much, you barely did anything?"

"Mrs. Jacobson I understand your grief, but you demanded an expensive CAT scan <u>and</u> extra lab tests."

188. ☆ ☆ ☆ ☆ ☆ ☆ ☆ ☆ ☆

Old Mr. Horowitz is in his hospital room after surgery. He is very tired and his throat is raspy because of the breathing tube. The young nurse comes in to check on him and Mr. Horowitz groans, "Are my testicles black?"

"What?" the young nurse says.

"Are my testicles black?" whispers Mr. Horowitz.

"I'm sure you're fine," says the nurse.

"Are my testicles black?"

"Mr. Horowitz, I'm sure you're just fine down there," she says nervously.

"Are my testicles black?" Mr. Horowitz struggles to say while getting frustrated.

Wanting to keep her patient calm, the nurse gently pulls back the covers and lifts his gown. "Everything looks fine, you need to rest."

Even more frustrated, Mr. Horowitz grabs a pad of paper and a pencil from the phone table and writes, "Are my test results back?"

When telling this joke, you want your audience to kind of hear, but not quite hear, Mr. Horowitz's garbled message.

"I offer this evidence of the Big Bang, brought to our attention by Sister Sullivan of Roanoke, New Jersey."

189. ☆ ☆ ☆ ☆ ☆ ☆ ☆ ☆ ☆

Over the years I have worked with a lot of veterans, this next joke was very popular right after the first Gulf War:
A division of Saddam Hussein's Republican Guard was out conducting advanced training deep in the desert. The commanding general noticed a single American soldier walking atop a sand dune.

The general ordered an elite guardsman to go kill the infidel.

The Iraqi soldier chased the American soldier over the dune and out of sight.

After a few minutes, the general yelled at his command, "How hard is it to kill one infidel!" Three Iraqi soldiers ran off over the dune to kill the infidel.

After a more few minutes, the general was furious, and ordered three platoons to get the job done.

After ten minutes passed, the general ordered the rest of his men, 314 in total, "to bring back the infidel's head!"

Just then the first Iraqi soldier stumbled back over the dune, he was bleeding and in shock as he waved his hands and yelled to the general, "Stop! It's a trap, there are two of them!"

190.   ☆ ☆ ☆ ☆ ☆ ☆ ☆ ☆ ☆ ☆

Yo momma's so fat when she sat on your pet rock she killed it!

191.   ☆ ☆ ☆ ☆ ☆ ☆ ☆ ☆ ☆ ☆

If at first you don't succeed… stay away from skydiving.

192.   ☆ ☆ ☆ ☆ ☆ ☆ ☆ ☆ ☆ ☆

Hanna calls her mother to confess her problem, "Ma, I met a boy," she says. "He's a nice boy, even if he isn't Jewish. He's from a nice family, even if his father is in the federal penitentiary for polygamy."

"What you saying?" Hanna's mother gasps.

"My new boyfriend is a nice boy, his family is Mormon and his father is getting out in just three years."

"Hanna, I don't understand what you are saying."

"The nice boy and I only had sex once." Hanna said. "We didn't mean to, but ma, I'm pregnant."

"Pregnant?" Hanna's mother screams. "What are you trying to do? Kill me!"

"No mom, it's all right. I'm really not pregnant. There is no boy or any of that," Hanna says.

"Oy, I'm almost dead. So what did you called for?" Hanna's

mother said.

"Ma, I'm in the Dean's office and he's forcing me to tell you that I'm failing Psychology."

193.　　　☆ ☆ ☆ ☆ ☆ ☆ ☆ ☆ ☆ ☆

A thug breaks into a really big house in the dead of night. He is looking around with his flashlight when he hears, "God is watching."

He shines his light all over but sees no one. Then, again out of the dark, he hears, "God is watching."

The shaken burglar turns quickly and finds a parrot, "Damn Polly," he laughs, "you scared me."

"Call me John the Baptist," squawks the parrot, "God is watching."

"Who in his right mind would name a parrot, John the Baptist?" laughs the burglar.

"Squawk, the same person who named the Rottweiler behind you, God."

194. ☆ ☆ ☆ ☆ ☆ ☆ ☆ ☆ ☆ ☆

The patient told his psychologist about his most recent dreams.

"I had a very vivid dream that I was a wigwam, you know the kind of tent Indians used to live in. Then I had a dream that I was a giant circus tent, with elephants and tigers."

The psychologist finished writing his notes then looked up, "It seems you are two tents."

195. ☆ ☆ ☆ ☆ ☆ ☆ ☆ ☆ ☆ ☆

A man walks into a shrink's office. He has a banana stuck up his nose and a watermelon rind for a hat. In one ear he has a grape, in the other what looks like mashed potatoes.

"I don't feel so good doc," he says, "what's wrong with me?"

The psychiatrist says, "It looks like you're not eating properly."

196. ☆ ☆ ☆ ☆ ☆ ☆ ☆ ☆ ☆ ☆

What's the gunk between elephant's toes?
Slow running natives.

197. ☆ ☆ ☆ ☆ ☆ ☆ ☆ ☆ ☆ ☆

Friends from college met at the reunion. One went on and on about his accomplishments.

"I ended up in the cattle business," he said as he puffed out his chest. "Now I own 20 thousand acres of prime Texas bottom land. You could ride all day in one of my many trucks and you still couldn't drive from one end to the other."

"I remember when I was poor," the other friend said, "I had a pick-up like that myself."

198. ☆ ☆ ☆ ☆ ☆ ☆ ☆ ☆ ☆ ☆

This next joke is a visual joke. It works best in front of an audience when you role play the action in the punch line.

My friend Reggie Bluff is not the brightest bulb on the tree. One day he was being driven crazy by his children so he decided to get some help from his doctor.

"Doc," Reggie confessed, "me and Ma have had 11 kids in just 10 years. Them there kids are driving me around the bend. I don't want no more kids!"

"I understand," the doctor said calmly. "Maybe it's time for you to get a vasectomy."

"Yeah, that's what I want," agreed Reggie. "But you know I ain't got much money. How much?"

"It'll cost you about ten thousand dollars."

"Ten thousand dollars, I ain't got no ten thousand dollars!"

"Well we can always get you an Arkansas vasectomy. That only costs a few dollars," said the doctor.

"OK, that's for me," nodded Reggie.

"All you have to do is go to the hardware store and buy a can of coke and a stick of dynamite. Then you go into your backyard all by yourself, drink the coke and light the dynamite. You put the dynamite into the can of coke and count to 10."

Reggie understood and off to the store he went.

Later that night, when the kids were all in bed, Reggie went out into the backyard, drank the coke, lit the dynamite and stuck it into the empty can. With the can in one hand he started to count on his fingers... 1,2,3,4,5... Then he realized he needed his other hand so he scooted that can way up between his legs... 6, 7, 8.

199.

Let's try another visual joke.

Reggie Bluff was as dumb as a box of hair. Back when he was in the Navy he was out at sea so long he developed 'sea legs'. That's what they call it when your legs get comfortable with the ship tossing port and starboard. The problem was when he got back on shore. He was so used to having sea legs that he lost his land legs and a chubby Irish cop thought he was walking all drunk.

Reggie tried to explain about his legs and that he wasn't drunk, but the fact that he was bobbing and weaving and almost falling down made the fat Irish cop even more convinced he was a stinking, lying, drunk.

In fact, the more Reggie tried to explain, the angrier the cop got.

Finally the cop growled at him and started to thrust his massive hips back and forth parading around like a sexed crazed maniac.

"Me and the misses have 14 children and you don't see me walking around like this do ya!"

200. ☆ ☆ ☆ ☆ ☆ ☆ ☆ ☆ ☆

Yo sister's so ugly yo momma has to tie a pork chop around her neck just to get the dog to play with her.

201. ☆ ☆ ☆ ☆ ☆ ☆ ☆ ☆ ☆

Bob: Did you hear they cancelled cheerleading at Red Bluff High?
Tom: No. How come?

Bob: They couldn't stop the girls from grazing during half time.

202. ☆ ☆ ☆ ☆ ☆ ☆ ☆ ☆

It's career day at the high school and Mr. Thompson finds himself running late and a little nervous. He knows he is a good Certified Public Accountant, but having to get up in front of hundreds of teens and hold their attention feels a little overwhelming. To make things worse, a few years ago during career day he had to give his *Why I became and accountant* speech right after a fireman talked about the rush of saving lives.

Mr. Thompson was told he was up next so he went into the large auditorium to wait his turn. On stage there was an old mangled sailor. He had an eye patch, a huge scar on his cheek, a hooked hand, and a wooden leg.

After he was done talking about his 40 years at sea he entertained questions.

"I don't want to be rude, but how did you lose your leg, hand, and eye?" asked a student.

The auditorium was silent.

The sailor looked at the boy with his one good eye and said, "Well matey, it's dangerous at sea."

"I lost my leg off the coast of Australia, during World War II, while trying to escape a Nazi U-boat when my ship scraped the Great Barrier Reef. Many good men lost their lives to great white sharks that day. I was one of the lucky ones."

"I lost my hand some ten years later. There was an engine fire and the captain ordered me to put it out. Many good men lost their lives that day. I was one of the lucky ones," he said as he waved his hook towards the boy.

"Sir," the student asked. "How'd you lose your eye?"

"That happen the same day I got fitted with my new hook. I was standing on deck and a pigeon pooped in my eye so I went and wiped the poop out of my eye forgetting about my new hook."

Mr. Thompson, CPA quietly left and went home.

203. ☆ ☆ ☆ ☆ ☆ ☆ ☆ ☆

A police officer spots a car swerving all over the street. He attempts to pull it over but the driver doesn't respond. He doesn't have a choice but to speed up alongside the car to get the driver's attention. To his surprise the driver is a little old lady peacefully knitting.

"Pull over, pull over," the cop yells.

"No," yells back the little old lady, "scarf"!

204. ☆ ☆ ☆ ☆ ☆ ☆ ☆ ☆ ☆

The first sentence of this joke is in the kid section. The complete joke works well with teens.

Mom says to dad, "I'm worried about our son. He named his new pet hamster, 'Goldfish'."

"He get's that from your side of the family," smirks dad.

"My side, what do you mean by that?"

"I'm not trying to start an argument, but you named last night's dinner 'meatloaf'."

"Tonight, I name the couch 'your bed'!"

Often I am told by teens, "My parents have real arguments just like this."

205. ☆ ☆ ☆ ☆ ☆ ☆ ☆ ☆ ☆

A bear goes into a tavern and sits at the bar and says, "I'd like ---------- a ---------- beer and a -------------- bag of nuts."

"Sure," smiles the bartender, "but what's with the big pause?"

206. ☆ ☆ ☆ ☆ ☆ ☆ ☆ ☆ ☆

Ms. Ames was trying to motivate her third graders to bring in their class picture money.

"Thirty years from now you will look at your class picture and say, 'There's my friend Susie, she's the president of the bank. There's my friend Bobby, he's a congressman now.'"

A little girl in the back of the class started to cry. "Becky, what's wrong?" Ms. Ames asked.

Pretending to point at a picture in her hand Becky sobbed, "There's Ms. Ames, she's dead now!"

"Your handwriting is so bad, that even though you emailed me your homework I still can't read it!"

207. ☆ ☆ ☆ ☆ ☆ ☆ ☆ ☆ ☆ ☆

Yo sister's so dumb, she named her pet zebra, spot!

208. ☆ ☆ ☆ ☆ ☆ ☆ ☆ ☆ ☆ ☆

The maintenance man at Central Park Zoo barged into the zoo director's office.

"Someone keeps stealing all the Hefty garbage liners from the trash cans all over the zoo!"

The zoo director, looking horrified grabs his phone and dials furiously.

"Yes, Veterinary Supplies? I need a rush order on 20 cases of elephant condoms! Hurry!"

209. ☆ ☆ ☆ ☆ ☆ ☆ ☆ ☆ ☆ ☆

Mortimer is about as quick as a box of no-legged turtles. One day he goes into the pharmacy and asks for some condoms.

"That will be $6.99 plus tax."

"Oh I don't want that. Don't you have the kind that stay on by themselves?"

210. ☆ ☆ ☆ ☆ ☆ ☆ ☆ ☆ ☆ ☆

It was 1885 and out west in a small mining town a miner needed to hire some help. He put an ad in the county's only newspaper, *The Craigslist and Fish Wrap*.

Only three prospects showed up, two old drunks and a young well educated Chinese exchange student.

The miner hired the three and assigned them their jobs. The first old drunk he gave a pick, the second he gave a wheelbarrow.

He turned to the Chinese exchange student and said, "You're in charge of supplies."

A week goes by and the miner rides on over to see how the new employees were getting along. He finds the two drunks hiding behind a big rock. They looked petrified.

"What ya doing?" barked the mine owner. "Why ain't you digging in the mine?"

"We ain't going in there," whispered the first drunk.

Not sure what was going on the miner pulled out his six gun and crept into the mine.

Just then the Chinese exchange student jumped out of the mine shaft and yelled, "Supplies!"

211. ☆ ☆ ☆ ☆ ☆ ☆ ☆ ☆ ☆ ☆

This next joke can be told almost as a G rated joke or a PG rated joke depending on your audience.

I once told this joke to a Sunday school teacher who was

telling me about the horrible carnage she saw in a PBS animal documentary:

"It is so sad that the big mean animals eat the little animals," she said.

"That reminds me of a story I heard about a bear and a bunny rabbit," I started.

"There was this bear," I looked around making sure we were not being overheard. "Well, he was crouched down doing what bears do in the woods, when this cute little bunny rabbit hopped on by. The bear said in a deep scary bear voice, 'Mr. Bunny, when you poop, do you get poop stuck to your fur?'"

"No, never do," said the cute little bunny.

So the bear wiped his bum with the rabbit.

She snickered, and a few seconds later the Sunday school teacher said, "You see, even in stories the big animals are mean to the little ones."

The same story for a more open minded audience. I still tell it with the character voices as if it is a bedtime story:

A bear was pooping in the woods when a bunny hopped on by.

The bear said to the bunny, "When you poop, do you get poop stuck in your fur?"

"No," said the bunny.

"So the bear wiped his ass with the bunny."

I have caught teens off guard many times with this joke, giving them a great laugh. The soft beginning with the sudden punchline is a winner with smart teens.

212.   ☆ ☆ ☆ ☆ ☆ ☆ ☆ ☆ ☆ ☆

Yo momma's so stupid she got locked overnight in a mattress store and slept on the floor.

213.   ☆ ☆ ☆ ☆ ☆ ☆ ☆ ☆ ☆ ☆

Yo momma's so stupid she could trip over a cordless phone!

214. ☆ ☆ ☆ ☆ ☆ ☆ ☆ ☆ ☆

What do you call cheese that isn't yours?
Nacho cheese.

"What makes you think 'cereal killer'?"

215. ☆ ☆ ☆ ☆ ☆ ☆ ☆ ☆ ☆

News Release:

Linda Thompson, one of the singers of the 1975 hit, The Hokey Pokey, died over the weekend. Her publicist said, "The funeral was a somber occasion limited to close friends and family. Unfortunately, laughter broke out during the viewing when officials attempted to put Mrs. Thompson's left foot in the casket, then her right foot in… you probably know the rest."

216.   ☆ ☆ ☆ ☆ ☆ ☆ ☆ ☆ ☆ ☆

A panda meets a nice girl at a bar. They hit it off really well and the nice girl invites the panda to her apartment for dinner.

One thing leads to another and the panda ends up staying the night, it is fair to say that there was pandemonium all night long.

In the morning the panda is getting ready to leave and the nice girl says, "You do know I'm a prostitute."

"What's a prostitute?" asks the panda.

The prostitute hands him a dictionary and tells him to look it up.

"Prostitute, a person who accepts money for sex," reads the panda. "That's interesting, but I'm a panda… look it up."

The prostitute looks up panda in the dictionary and reads it out loud. "Panda, eats shoots, and leaves."

Jokes that are play on words tend to be very funny to teen minds as they juxtapose grammatical rules. Let's try another one.

217.   ☆ ☆ ☆ ☆ ☆ ☆ ☆ ☆ ☆ ☆

Punctuation counts:

Let's eat grandma.
Let's eat, grandma.

I helped my Uncle Jack off a horse."
I helped my uncle jack off a horse.

King George walked and talked an hour after his head was cut off.
King George walked and talked, an hour after, his head was cut off.

I'd like to thank my parents, Ayn Rand and God.
I'd like to thank my parents, Ayn Rand, and God.

Woman, without her, man is nothing.
Woman, without her man, is nothing.

218.

I am very fond of dangling modifiers. So here are a few I adore:

- Hanging from my dresser drawer I found my sock.
- Police found safe under bed.
- Hanging on the wall, my mom really liked the picture.
- Baking in the oven, Phil waited for the pizza.
- The woman walked the dog in red cowboy boots.
- Covered in mustard and relish, Geri enjoyed the hot dog.

219.

A new guy in town gets himself invited to the friendly poker game in the back of the small town police station. When he gets there, he is surprised to see Roscoe, the police dog, playing poker with the guys.

"Is the dog any good at poker?" the new guy asks.

"No," says the police chief, "every time he gets a good hand he wags his tail."

220.

A handsome prince of a frog hopped into a bank looking for a loan.

"Welcome sir," said Mrs. Patty Whack, the loan officer.

"I would like a loan," the frog said.

"I'm sorry sir, we do not loan money to frogs," explained Mrs. Whack.

"I want to talk to the bank manager!" demanded the frog.

The bank manager came over and was told what was going on.

"It is unusual," said the bank manager. "Do you have any collateral?"

"Yes," said the frog. Then he took off his hat and showed the bank manager a very fragile figurine of a cute bunny rabbit.

"What is that?" said the loan officer to the bank manager.

"That's a nick-knack Patty Whack, give this frog a loan."

221. ☆ ☆ ☆ ☆ ☆ ☆ ☆ ☆ ☆ ☆

Life is a sexually transmitted disease.

222. ☆ ☆ ☆ ☆ ☆ ☆ ☆ ☆ ☆ ☆

About halfway through the show, a drunk in the audience yells at the ventriloquist, "Stop making so may Polish jokes, I'm Polish and I don't find them funny!"

"Calm down friend," the ventriloquists says, "they're just jokes... lighten up a bit."

"I'm not talking to you," the drunk yells, "I'm talking to that little fellow on your lap!"

223.

What do you call a cow with no legs?
Ground beef!

224.

Why did the pervert cross the road?
Because he was looking for a chicken.

225.

Sterility is hereditary: If your grandfather didn't have children and your father didn't have children, you will not be able to have children.

226.

Angry teens tend to tell me this joke:

Why did the pervert cross the road?
Because his weenie was stuck in a chicken.

227.

Did you hear about the kamikaze pilot who flew 54 missions? His name was Chicken Teriyaki.

228.

An English gentleman in the heat of sexual passion came to an abrupt halt.
"Are you all right," he asked his wife. "Did I hurt you?"
"No. Not at all," she breathed. "Why did you ask?"
"I thought you moved."

229.

Recently a teenager in my office was trying to get my goat. He patted me on my ample tummy and said, "You should diet".

"I agree," I smiled, "what color?"

230. ☆ ☆ ☆ ☆ ☆ ☆ ☆ ☆ ☆ ☆

Mrs. Jacobson was taking a shower when the doorbell rang. Peeking out the window she saw the brown delivery truck. Her important package had finally arrived.

She hastily wrapped a towel around her lower body and another around her upper. Making sure she was completely covered, she went to the front door. While signing for the package, Mrs. Jacobson was startled by her cat running through her legs. This made her lose her balance for a moment and her upper towel accidentally slipped off.

She was horrified and screamed at the cat, "SEYMOUR, SEYMOUR!" as she tried to cover herself.

The delivery man yelled back as he ran down the walkway, "No thanks lady, I've seen enough!"

231. ☆ ☆ ☆ ☆ ☆ ☆ ☆ ☆ ☆ ☆

I hear that yo momma is so ugly that yo father takes her to work with him just so he doesn't have to kiss her goodbye.

232. ☆ ☆ ☆ ☆ ☆ ☆ ☆ ☆ ☆ ☆

Yo momma's so skinny that when she went to prison her uniform only had one stripe.

233. ☆ ☆ ☆ ☆ ☆ ☆ ☆ ☆ ☆ ☆

Yo momma's so old that when she was young the Dead Sea just had a cold.

234. ☆ ☆ ☆ ☆ ☆ ☆ ☆ ☆ ☆ ☆

Mrs. Hollister went to the doctor.

"I have a problem with silent gas. It's very embarrassing. You probably have not noticed but I've passed gas three times since I've been in your exam room.

"THE FIRST THING WE NEED TO DO," the doctor said loudly, "IS TO GET YOUR EARS CHECKED."

235. ☆ ☆ ☆ ☆ ☆ ☆ ☆ ☆ ☆

Yo sister's so dumb that when she saw the sign, AIRPORT LEFT, she turned around and went home.

236. ☆ ☆ ☆ ☆ ☆ ☆ ☆ ☆ ☆

Yo momma's so fat that she can't even fit into an Internet chat room.

237. ☆ ☆ ☆ ☆ ☆ ☆ ☆ ☆ ☆

Is it true that yo momma's so short that she poses for trophies?

238. ☆ ☆ ☆ ☆ ☆ ☆ ☆ ☆ ☆

Is it true that yo momma's so fat that when she goes to the zoo the elephants throw peanuts at her?

239. ☆ ☆ ☆ ☆ ☆ ☆ ☆ ☆ ☆

Yo momma's so ugly her psychiatrist makes her lie on the couch face down.

240. ☆ ☆ ☆ ☆ ☆ ☆ ☆ ☆ ☆

Yo momma's so ugly even the Womping Willow wouldn't hit that!

"Damn the FBI warning... We want all your DVD's now!"

241. ☆ ☆ ☆ ☆ ☆ ☆ ☆ ☆ ☆ ☆

Yo brother's so ugly he looks like he plays goalie for the dart team.

242. ☆ ☆ ☆ ☆ ☆ ☆ ☆ ☆ ☆ ☆

Yo momma's so ugly that when she looks in a mirror her reflections ducks.

243. ☆ ☆ ☆ ☆ ☆ ☆ ☆ ☆ ☆ ☆

Yo daddy drinks so much that his red nose can stop traffic.

244. ☆ ☆ ☆ ☆ ☆ ☆ ☆ ☆ ☆ ☆

Yo momma's so old she farts dust.

245. ☆ ☆ ☆ ☆ ☆ ☆ ☆ ☆ ☆ ☆

A blond young lady was pulled over for speeding by a cop, who also happened to be blond. The driver was having trouble finding her license in her little purse and accidentally handed the officer a small mirror.

After looking at the mirror, the police woman said, "Here's your license ma'am, you can go. You should have told me you were a cop."

246. ☆ ☆ ☆ ☆ ☆ ☆ ☆ ☆ ☆ ☆

In California everyone practically lives in their cars. Now there is a new company franchising drive-through funeral homes called, Jump In The Box.

247. ☆ ☆ ☆ ☆ ☆ ☆ ☆ ☆ ☆ ☆

I'm not saying yo momma's fat, but she has more chins than a Chinese phonebook.

248. ☆ ☆ ☆ ☆ ☆ ☆ ☆ ☆ ☆ ☆

Did you know that Abraham Lincoln was Jewish?
Everyone knows he was shot in the temple.

249. ☆ ☆ ☆ ☆ ☆ ☆ ☆ ☆ ☆ ☆

Did you hear that they figured out why the catbird went extinct?
Scientist figured it's because its mating call was, "Here kitty, kitty, here kitty, kitty".

250. ☆ ☆ ☆ ☆ ☆ ☆ ☆ ☆ ☆ ☆

Did you hear about the cannibal who was expelled from school for buttering up his teacher?

251. ☆ ☆ ☆ ☆ ☆ ☆ ☆ ☆ ☆ ☆

You're so ugly that when you were born the doctor slapped yo momma.

252. ☆ ☆ ☆ ☆ ☆ ☆ ☆ ☆ ☆

If my dog was as ugly as you, I'd shave its butt and teach him to walk backwards!

E-mail: President George Bush
From: Danny "The Roach" Thompson

Dear Mr. President,

I have a really big problem. I need your help. When I called my mom from school, She said I could go over to Tony's house. She said that she told me to be home by 8 O'clock. But she didn't. Now I'm grounded. Could you please ask the National Security Administration to check that call. I really want to go to the mall on Saturday.

Thanks a bunch dude,

The Roach

253. ☆ ☆ ☆ ☆ ☆ ☆ ☆ ☆ ☆

What do Hawaiian cows like to wear?
Moo moos.

254. ☆☆☆☆☆☆☆☆☆

What did the doe say when she came out of the woods?
I'll never do that again for 2 bucks!

255. ☆☆☆☆☆☆☆☆☆

Yo momma's house is so dirty, you have to wipe your feet just to go outside!

256. ☆☆☆☆☆☆☆☆☆

Yo momma's so fat she is half Irish, half Italian, and half Russian.

257. ☆☆☆☆☆☆☆☆☆

How much did the pirate pay for his earrings?
A buck an ear.

258. ☆☆☆☆☆☆☆☆☆

Yo momma's so fat her measurements are 36-24-36 and her other arm is even bigger.

259. ☆☆☆☆☆☆☆☆☆

Yo momma's so fat that when she gets on a scale it reads, GET OFF!

260. ☆☆☆☆☆☆☆☆☆

Yo momma's so fat that when she hauls ass it takes two trips.

261. ☆☆☆☆☆☆☆☆☆

Yo momma's so fat that her blood type is Ragu.

262. ☆ ☆ ☆ ☆ ☆ ☆ ☆ ☆ ☆

When I got up this morning I shot a bear in my pajamas. I wonder why he was in my pajamas?

263. ☆ ☆ ☆ ☆ ☆ ☆ ☆ ☆ ☆

Yo momma's so fat that when she went into the Gap, she filled it.

264. ☆ ☆ ☆ ☆ ☆ ☆ ☆ ☆ ☆

Yo momma's so fat that she has to fall to sleep in sections?

265. ☆ ☆ ☆ ☆ ☆ ☆ ☆ ☆ ☆

Yo momma's so fat that when she sat on a quarter a booger popped out of George Washington's nose.

266. ☆ ☆ ☆ ☆ ☆ ☆ ☆ ☆ ☆

I like to take my pet lion to church on Sundays. He's gotta eat!

267. ☆ ☆ ☆ ☆ ☆ ☆ ☆ ☆ ☆

Research has proven that half of all people are below average.

268. ☆ ☆ ☆ ☆ ☆ ☆ ☆ ☆ ☆

Yo daddy's got such a bad credit rating cashiers demand ID even when he's paying cash.

269. ☆ ☆ ☆ ☆ ☆ ☆ ☆ ☆ ☆

A farmer was stuck by the side of the interstate after his old truck pooped out on him. A man in a magnificent Ferrari pulled up to help. Within minutes it was obvious to both men that the old truck needed a real mechanic. So the Ferrari owner offered to tow the farmer's truck.

As the Ferrari and old truck were moving down the road, a Porsche pulled up alongside the Ferrari and some disparaging remarks were exchanged. Within moments they were hitting breakneck speeds.

A motorcycle cop caught them on radar and couldn't believe what he just saw. He radioed dispatch, "I need backup, now! A Ferrari and a Porsche just flew by me at 216 miles per hour, and an old Chevy truck was honking furiously at 'em to let 'em pass!"

270. ☆ ☆ ☆ ☆ ☆ ☆ ☆ ☆ ☆

Why do we call it rush hour when nothing's moving?

271. ☆ ☆ ☆ ☆ ☆ ☆ ☆ ☆ ☆

Yo momma's so fat her shadow weighs 216 pounds.

272. ☆ ☆ ☆ ☆ ☆ ☆ ☆ ☆ ☆

How many IRS agents does it take to screw in a lightbulb?
Only one... but it really gets screwed.

273. ☆ ☆ ☆ ☆ ☆ ☆ ☆ ☆ ☆

How many real men does it take to change a lightbulb?
None. Real men aren't afraid of the dark.

274. ☆ ☆ ☆ ☆ ☆ ☆ ☆ ☆ ☆

How many Irish men does it take to change a lightbulb?
Ten. One to hold the bulb and nine to drink until the room spins.

275. ☆ ☆ ☆ ☆ ☆ ☆ ☆ ☆ ☆

If we're not suppose to eat animals, why are they made out of meat?

276.   ☆ ☆ ☆ ☆ ☆ ☆ ☆ ☆ ☆

Yo momma's so fat she doesn't use a fork, she uses a forklift!

277.   ☆ ☆ ☆ ☆ ☆ ☆ ☆ ☆ ☆

Yo momma's so fat she puts her lipstick on with a paint roller.

278.   ☆ ☆ ☆ ☆ ☆ ☆ ☆ ☆ ☆

In the old days when telegrams were seen as very important, and usually meant something bad had occurred, a principal read out a telegram in front of the school assembly, addressed to an unknown teacher. It was his hope that the right person would come forward.

"Dear honey not getting any better come home soon Maggy"

Not sure about the punctuation, he tries it again.

"Dear Honey, Not getting any better, come home soon. Maggy"

Finally, the janitor comes forward, takes the paper, and adds a few marks.

The principal reads the telegraph again.

"Dear Honey, Not getting any. Better come home soon. Maggy."

279.   ☆ ☆ ☆ ☆ ☆ ☆ ☆ ☆ ☆

The wealthy businessman was a little putout when a bum asked him for $10 for coffee.

"Ten dollars for coffee, that's outrageous, you can get coffee for much less than that!" the business man yelled.

"I know that," the bum said calmly, "but you don't want me to skimp on the tip just because I'm a little down on my luck do ya?"

280.   ☆ ☆ ☆ ☆ ☆ ☆ ☆ ☆ ☆

Mrs. St. James, dressed in diamonds and furs, was running late for a Republican presidential fundraiser, when a bum stopped her in the street.

"Lady, a little help," he said as he held his hand out, "I haven't eaten in 3 days."

"Well," Mrs. St. James said in a concerned tone, "you really should force yourself."

"Do you really think it was a good idea to flush the toilet during your phone interview!"

281. ☆ ☆ ☆ ☆ ☆ ☆ ☆ ☆ ☆ ☆

Mr. Rosenbaum decided to lose weight so he went to a weight loss clinic that was getting good results. He paid an exorbitant amount of money and was told that everyday he would have to go to room 102. The first day he went to his assigned room, which was a gymnasium, and he sat on a small stool awaiting his instructor. Looking around, he was very concerned about having to lift weights or run around a lot. After a few minutes, a tall blond woman wearing short shorts and half a top came in and said, "If you can catch me you can have me!"

It was amazing, in no time he lost 12 pounds with the blond. He lost another 8 pounds with the brunette, and 12 pounds with the redhead.

But, after 3 weeks Mr. Rosenbaum still needed to lose another 50 pounds, so he paid a lot more money to take the advanced weight loss course.

On his first day in the advanced course he was lead to a very large gymnasium where he sat on a small stool awaiting his "weight loss instructor".

After a few minutes, a large angry looking fat man entered the room and proceeded to put a chain on the door, padlocking it securely. In a deep voice he said to Mr. Rosenbaum, "If I can catch you, I can have you!"

282. ☆ ☆ ☆ ☆ ☆ ☆ ☆ ☆ ☆

Yo momma's so fat she's my two best friends.

283. ☆ ☆ ☆ ☆ ☆ ☆ ☆ ☆ ☆

Two cows were standing around grazing when one said to the other, "What do you think about this Mad Cow disease?"

The other cow flapped her ears frantically and rolled her eyes in a tizzy while saying, "What do I care, I'm a helicopter."

284. ☆ ☆ ☆ ☆ ☆ ☆ ☆ ☆ ☆

A man, wearing jumper cables dangling from his neck, goes into a bar and orders a beer.

The bartender puts a beer in front of him and says, "Don't start anything."

285. ☆ ☆ ☆ ☆ ☆ ☆ ☆ ☆ ☆

A man was at the cash register buying a six pack of beer and a frozen dinner. The cashier said, "You're single aren't you?"

"Yes, how did you know?"

The cashier leaned forward and whispered, "Because you're ugly."

286. ☆ ☆ ☆ ☆ ☆ ☆ ☆ ☆ ☆

Ralph goes into Momma's Restaurant looking forward to a bowl of Momma's Famous Homemade Chili. He was disappointed when he was told by the waitress that they were all out. While looking over the menu he noticed that the guy at the next table was engrossed in his iPad and hadn't touched his chili.

"Excuse me," Ralph asked, "do you mind if I eat your bowl of chili? I was really looking forward to Momma's chili today."

"OK with me," the other guy glanced up and said.

About halfway into the bowl of chili Ralph came upon a dead mouse and threw up back into the bowl.

"That's as far as I got, too!" the other guy said.

287. ☆ ☆ ☆ ☆ ☆ ☆ ☆ ☆ ☆

What sits in the kitchen and keeps getting smaller and smaller?
A baby combing its hair with a potato peeler.

288. ☆ ☆ ☆ ☆ ☆ ☆ ☆ ☆ ☆

What does the art school grad say to the engineering school grad?
"Do you want fries with that, sir?"

289. ☆ ☆ ☆ ☆ ☆ ☆ ☆ ☆ ☆

After graduating from college, what does the English major say to the engineering major?
"So here's a Grande Double Mocha Latte, anything else, sir?"

290. ☆ ☆ ☆ ☆ ☆ ☆ ☆ ☆ ☆

Billy Bob called 911. "Hurry, momma's having a heart attack."
"What is your location?" dispatch asked.
"We're at home," said Billy Bob.
"Yes sir, what is the address?"
"It's 37 Eucalyptus Street," said Billy Bob.
"How do you spell that?" asked dispatch.
"AHH, That's ah u-c-a-l... How about I drag momma over to Oak Street?

291. ☆ ☆ ☆ ☆ ☆ ☆ ☆ ☆ ☆

Mr. Goldberg called Mr. Levi, the undertaker, and asked him to take care of all the arrangements for his wife's funeral.

"But Mr. Goldberg," Levi asked, "Didn't I bury your wife some ten years ago?"

"Sure you did, and you did a wonderful job, but I got remarried last month, and unfortunately my second wife just passed."

"Congratulations," said Mr Levi.

292. ☆ ☆ ☆ ☆ ☆ ☆ ☆ ☆ ☆

My friend Martin is blind. One day I asked him if he knew that there was braille on the driver up ATMs at the bank. He said that he had heard about that, but asked if I knew that there was braille on lady's bodies.

"No," I said.

"Well there is," he joked, "Those bumps around her nipples read, 'lick here'."

293. ☆ ☆ ☆ ☆ ☆ ☆ ☆ ☆ ☆

What were the final words Jesus spoke at the Last Supper?

"Anyone who wants to be in the picture, come to this side of the table."

294. ☆ ☆ ☆ ☆ ☆ ☆ ☆ ☆ ☆

This joke takes a hand gesture. So at the appropriate time, hold your thumb and forefinger 2 inches apart.

Why do woman have such difficulty parking? It's not because of hand eye coordination or basic intelligence. I figure it's because they have been told so often that <u>this</u> is 8 inches.

295. ☆ ☆ ☆ ☆ ☆ ☆ ☆ ☆ ☆

A man goes to the dentist because of a really bad toothache. "How much to pull this tooth, doc?"

"$195."

"$195 for just a minute's work?" the patient complains.

"If you want," the dentist says, "I can pull it very slowly."

296. ☆☆☆☆☆☆☆☆☆

A doctor calls up the plumber to complain about the bill. "You charged me $400 to fix one toilet? It only took you 10 minutes!"

"Yeah," said the plumber.

"That's outrageous! I went to medical school and I don't charge that much."

"I know," said the plumber, "that's why I dropped out of medical school."

297. ☆☆☆☆☆☆☆☆☆

What is the worst part about killing someone?
Getting blood on your clown suit.

298. ☆☆☆☆☆☆☆☆☆

Did you hear about the guy who had sex with his canary? They say he came down with an untweetable case of churpies.

299. ☆☆☆☆☆☆☆☆☆

I once dated a girl who wasn't too smart when it came to cars. After I replaced the blinker fuse I asked her to see if it was working.

I sat in the driver's seat and turned it on, while she stood in back of the car yelling to me, "it's on, it's off, it's on, it's off, it's on, it's off..."

300. ☆☆☆☆☆☆☆☆☆

A little more word play:

Drink up, Chuck and Die.
Drink, upchuck, and Die.

Those old things in the attic are my husband's.
Those old things in the attic are my husbands.

301. ☆ ☆ ☆ ☆ ☆ ☆ ☆ ☆ ☆

What's green and red and goes nowhere in a circle at fifty miles per hour?
A frog in a blender.

302. ☆ ☆ ☆ ☆ ☆ ☆ ☆ ☆ ☆

Newspaper headline:

Police Recruit Dead

303. ☆ ☆ ☆ ☆ ☆ ☆ ☆ ☆ ☆

Which is easier to unload, a truckload of bowling balls or a truck load of dead babies?
Dead babies, because you can use a pitchfork.

304. ☆ ☆ ☆ ☆ ☆ ☆ ☆ ☆ ☆

The Oow-Ah bird gets its name because it lays square eggs. Oooow aaaaaaaaaaah!

305. ☆ ☆ ☆ ☆ ☆ ☆ ☆ ☆ ☆

A grasshopper goes into a bar and the bartender says, "Hey, we have a drink named after you."
"That's weird," says the grasshopper. "Why would anyone name a drink Juan Carlos Rodriguez Hilario Javier Smyth III.

306. ☆ ☆ ☆ ☆ ☆ ☆ ☆ ☆ ☆

Did you know that Arkansas is the only state that doesn't allow workers to take coffee breaks?

It's too hard to retrain them.

307. ☆ ☆ ☆ ☆ ☆ ☆ ☆ ☆ ☆

Bob and Jake have been best friends since law school. On this day they are in the ocean snorkeling when they spot an enormous great white shark circling. Bob pulls a small penknife and Jake says, "You can't fight that thing, we gotta out swim it!"

"I don't have to out swim the shark," Bob said as he stabbed Jake in the leg. "I just have to out swim you!"

308. ☆ ☆ ☆ ☆ ☆ ☆ ☆ ☆ ☆

Bubba Dumnbucket takes his son hunting for the first time.

"Son," Dumnbucket says, "We're going to do whatever it takes to bag you a bear. Bears are dangerous business, but you can't be a real man until you kill yourself a bear. You're growing up son, this here's a rite of passage. Do you understand me son?"

"I think so pa. But, if the bear kills you… how do I get home for supper?"

309. ☆ ☆ ☆ ☆ ☆ ☆ ☆ ☆ ☆

A very drunk wife said to her very drunk husband, "You're the man I'm planning to grow old, ugly, and stinky with."

310. ☆ ☆ ☆ ☆ ☆ ☆ ☆ ☆ ☆

Why do men from Arkansas get married?
Sheep can't cook.

311. ☆ ☆ ☆ ☆ ☆ ☆ ☆ ☆ ☆

During World War II many Americans opened their homes to soldiers, often offering Sunday dinner for the men faraway from their own families.

Mrs. Worthington wanted to do her part, so the week before Thanksgiving she called the local Army base and generously invited six soldiers for a fine home cooked feast.

As she made the arrangements with the sergeant, she made sure he understood, "Please, sergeant, no Jewish boys… I'm sure you understand."

At the appointed time, the doorbell rang and Mrs. Worthington was astonished to find six smartly uniformed black soldiers standing at attention on her front porch.

"Ah, Ah… there must be some mistake," Mrs. Worthington stammered.

"I wouldn't think so, ma'am," one soldier said, "Sergeant Cohen isn't known for making mistakes."

312.

☆ ☆ ☆ ☆ ☆ ☆ ☆ ☆

Jokes are a form of art, maybe a lower form, but a form nonetheless. As a form of art, jokes can be used to start a conversation or to allow a dialogue to occur on a difficult subject.

Often I discuss racism with teens by starting the discussion with one of the following 3 jokes:

Private Thompson and Private Washington were having a shouting match when the drill sergeant entered the barracks.

"What's the meaning of this?" the sergeant growled.

As the two men snapped to attention, Washington explained, "Sir sergeant sir, Thompson keeps giving me the worst jobs because

I'm black."

"Men," the sergeant said, "in this here army there are no black soldiers or white soldiers. There are only green soldiers. Now, I want the light green soldier mopping floors and the dark green soldier emptying trash!"

313. ☆ ☆ ☆ ☆ ☆ ☆ ☆ ☆ ☆ ☆

I like this next joke because it also looks at the power of words.

Little Bobby was helping his mother make dinner. When she looked away for a minute, Bobby smeared chocolate pudding all over his face and laughed, "Look mommy, I'm a nigger!"

Bobby's mother was furious and slapped Bobby hard upside his pudding covered face. "We don't use words like that young man," she screamed. "Go tell your father what you just did!"

Bobby did as he was told and his father was also furious. While he was severely spanking Bobby his father shouted, "You should know better than that. We do not use the n-word in this house! Go tell your grandfather what you have done."

Bobby did as he was told, and got another beating from his grandfather.

Bobby went back to the kitchen in tears where his mother said to him, "What did you learn young man?"

Bobby tried to control his sobs as he rubbed his bottom, "I leaned that I've only been black for 5 minutes and I already hate you white people!"

314. ☆ ☆ ☆ ☆ ☆ ☆ ☆ ☆ ☆ ☆

Did you hear about the hurricane that tore through New Jersey? It caused 28 million dollars in improvements.

315. ☆ ☆ ☆ ☆ ☆ ☆ ☆ ☆ ☆ ☆

Have you ever noticed that trailer parks are magnets for tornadoes?

316. ☆ ☆ ☆ ☆ ☆ ☆ ☆ ☆ ☆

If you are ever in Arkansas and see 100 John Deer tractors circling the McDonald's drive-through you'll know it's Prom Night.

317. ☆ ☆ ☆ ☆ ☆ ☆ ☆ ☆ ☆

One parent approached another parent at the school bus stop.

"I need to talk to you about your son," the parent said angrily, "It seems that your son is playing doctor with my Bethany!"

"It's normal for 7-year-olds to be curious about sex," the second parent smiled.

"Sex!" the first parent screamed. "He took out Bethany's appendix!"

318. ☆ ☆ ☆ ☆ ☆ ☆ ☆ ☆ ☆

I do not believe that there are bad words. Words are words. There are situations where you should self censor your language so not to offend others. But I see that as personal responsibility.

I would not swear in front of my mother because I know that she would be offended by such behavior. I heard Buddy Hackett[2] tell the following story:

Words aren't bad, they're just words. People get upset by words. Oh my gosh, you said 'ass' how vulgar. Ass is not a bad word. If a guy comes up to you with a gun and shoves it in your neck. He's a crazy looking guy. He has a big scar on his face, all gnarled... he is going to kill you. That's bad! That same man has that gun stuck up his ass, who cares...

---

[2] In my humble opinion, Buddy Hackett is the best storyteller I have ever heard. (Please don't tell my uncles.) You can find a few of his appearances from The Tonight Show with Johnny Carson on YouTube. I highly recommend you get a good laugh, then study his presentation skills. When he died in 2003, the New York Times wrote: *Buddy Hackett, the streetwise comedian from Brooklyn with a face like a plate of mashed potatoes, died yesterday at his beach house in Malibu, Calif. He was 78.*

Words are just words. Even the word 'fuck'. It is just a word. You drop an anvil on your foot, you don't say, 'how do you do?' No! You yell, 'FUCK!' You go to the emergency room with your foot all spread out, in pain and all broken. The doctor looks at it and says, 'You broke your fucking foot!' See that's even medical talk. If you drop an anvil on your foot you didn't just break your foot... you broke your fucking foot!

I have been a therapist for over 30 years. Some patients, especially the children, hang around in my psyche and reemerge as a cartoon character.

3. Jokes you should never tell children

I write jokes in plain English. It is too hard to read a joke written in broken English or with an accent. Before you tell this type of joke you need to practice the accents. For example, if it's a Jewish joke a particular cadence is needed and it's best to add a Yiddish accent. So, if the words are written as, "Well I said to the..." you say it as "Vell, I said to da...?" If you add arm gestures and facial expressions, you're on the way to the big times.

I was born into a Jewish home, and I must confess my favorite jokes are Jewish jokes. My uncles and aunts from the "old country" were funny people. My family used jokes to relieve tension and calm the rough waters of life. Because of my bias, you're about to read a lot of Jewish jokes. Then again, this might be good. How funny are the Syrians or the Bolivians anyway?

I do not believe in censorship except on a personal level. I don't want a government telling anybody what they can or cannot read. However, if locker room talk isn't funny to you, please stop reading now. If you have ever been offended please do not read any further.

If you are reading this you are in for some funny jokes.

319. ☆ ☆ ☆ ☆ ☆ ☆ ☆ ☆ ☆

For twenty-two years Mr. Braverman ate lunch at the same restaurant around the corner from his office. Everyday, corned beef on rye with a bowl of vegetable soup. He had been going there for so long, they had the soup and the sandwich ready when he arrived promptly at 12:06.

Everyday, Mr. Braverman ate his lunch with never a word. Twenty-two years never a, 'How you do' or 'nice day'.

Today Mr. Braverman came in and sat in front of his corned beef and soup. When the waiter went by, Mr. Braverman stopped him, "Taste my soup."

"Is there something wrong with the soup?" the waited asked.

"Taste my soup."

"I can't taste your soup, sir. Do you want me to get you another bowl?"

"Taste my soup."

"But sir, I can't, do you want a different kind?"

"Taste my soup."

The waiter was getting a little frustrated, so he relented.

"OK, I'll taste your soup." He looked around the table, "But sir, you don't have a spoon."

"Ahhh!" Mr. Braverman said as he wagged his finger.

"Do you want to play spin the bottle or be really nasty... I'll be a passenger and you can be a TSA agent."

320. ☆ ☆ ☆ ☆ ☆ ☆ ☆ ☆ ☆

My Uncle Sol was driving across the new bridge late last week and to his surprise he saw his friend Jacob climbing over the railing. He screeched to a halt and called to him, "Jacob, for God's sake what are you doing?"

"I want to die," Jacob said. "I've had enough all ready."

"But Jacob, you have so much to live for. What about your family and all your friends at the synagogue?"

"I know, I know," Jacob called back. "I built this bridge, I got the funding for this bridge… but does anyone say, 'There goes Jacob the bridge builder?'"

"Most of the buildings out there," Jacob pointed. "Most of those buildings—I was the chief architect. But do people say, There goes Jacob the architect?'"

"I've written six books on architecture, but do people say, 'There goes Jacob the author?'"

"No they don't! But… you suck one cock and all they say…"

321. ☆ ☆ ☆ ☆ ☆ ☆ ☆ ☆ ☆

Hymie told his oldest friend that he was marrying a 27 year old stripper from Poughkeepsie.

"But Hymie," his friend said, "you're 82 for God's sake!"

"So, I'm 82, I have needs. I have my health!"

"Sure," said his friend, "But what if on your honeymoon… during all that whoop-ti doop-ti… well you know——maybe a heart attack or a stroke, God forbid."

Hymie thought about it a minute, "Well, if she dies, she dies."

322. ☆ ☆ ☆ ☆ ☆ ☆ ☆ ☆ ☆

Uncle Sol was in a department store in downtown Miami. He walked up to a sales clerk and said, "I want to buy the store."

The clerk looked at him and realized he was serious, so he called the sales manager.

Uncle Sol turned to the sales manager and said, "I want to buy the store."

"What?" said the sales manager.

"I was reading the paper this morning, while I was having a bagel and lovely whitefish, and it said that this store might be for sale, So, I want to buy the store."

"Very good sir, But I can't sell you the store. Let me take you to the corporate office," said the sales manager.

The sales manager escorted Uncle Sol up to the corporate office on the fifth floor. The walls were mahogany, and the men and women were smartly dressed. Uncle Sol, wearing his old leisure suit looked a little out of place. Everyone was watching.

The sales manager introduced Uncle Sol to the president of the board's personal assistant and she took Uncle Sol into a huge office with paneled walls and elaborate paintings.

"I'm Henry Worthington the third," said the CEO while looking down his nose at Uncle Sol.

"Nice to meet you Mr. Third, I'd like to buy the store."

"What, what, what, buy my store?" said Henry Worthington the third.

"Yeah, I read in the paper that you folks are running on hard times and I have always wanted a store in Miami. I have a small place in the Bronx, but we are very crowded. I need more room. I want to buy the store."

"Sir, we are valued at $10 million dollars!"

"OK, $10 million it is, let me use the phone," said Uncle Sol.

"Sadie, it's Sol. Are you in the hotel room? Good, would you go look under the bed? You'll find two packages. You see them? Good... I need you to catch a cab and bring me the small one."

323.   ☆ ☆ ☆ ☆ ☆ ☆ ☆ ☆ ☆

Did you hear that at the start of the war in Iraq the French government heard that a war broke out?

Just to be safe, they surrendered.

324.   ☆ ☆ ☆ ☆ ☆ ☆ ☆ ☆ ☆

Uncle Sol was getting close to retirement. For over 50 years he had sold to every major store in the greater New York area. But, he had one nagging problem. There was this small chain in Albany that he visited once a month. They were rude to him and often slammed the door in his face yelling, "We don't do business with your kind!" But, it was on his route so he stopped by and tried again and again—every time he drove through Albany. In all that time they had never bought anything from him. He knew he couldn't retire until he sold them something.

So Uncle Sol went and camped in their purchasing agent's outer office for three days. Finally, Mr. Smyth let him have a meeting.

"I'm retiring soon," Uncle Sol said." And I don't want to go leaving any hard feelings. So please, buy something from me. You're the only company I have <u>never</u> sold anything to. You buy something, anything, and you will never have to see me darken your doorway again."

Mr. Smyth pulled himself up in his chair. "So, if I buy anything we're done forever?"

"Sure."

"What is the cheapest thing you sell?" asked Mr. Smyth.

"Well we have a lovely white ribbon, for you I can let you have it for just 18 cents a yard."

"Fine," Smyth said. "I'll make you a deal, just to get rid of you I'll buy a piece of ribbon as long as the distance from the tip of your nose to the tip of your pecker! That's it, take it or leave it!"

"OK," said Uncle Sol. I'll write up the purchase order, exactly what you say. Then you will never have to deal with me again."

A few weeks later, Mr. Smyth was in his office and heard truck after truck pulling into the loading dock. He was furious when he found out Uncle Sol had 18 truckloads of ribbon delivered.

In a rage, he got Uncle Sol on the phone. "What the hell game are you up to? I didn't order 18 truck loads of ribbon from you."

"Ah, nice to hear from you Mr. Smyth. I have your purchase order right here in front of me. Yes, I see you signed it and I wrote it up exactly as you ordered, "White Ribbon. Length: Tip of Sol's nose to tip of Sol's penis. Yes we delivered it right Mr. Smyth. Exactly what you ordered."

"The paperwork sounds right, so why did you send me so much ribbon?" Mr Smyth sputtered.

"Well Mr. Smyth, I'm sure I measured it correctly. My nose is here in New York City and the tip of my putz is in Warsaw, Poland."

"Ken loved napping by the glow of his highly monetized website"

325. ☆ ☆ ☆ ☆ ☆ ☆ ☆ ☆ ☆

This quote sounds like something my old uncles would have said.

Pope John XXIII said, "God knew from all eternity that I was going to be Pope. You would think he would have made me more photogenic."

326. ☆☆☆☆☆☆☆☆☆

Harry is constantly complaining to his wife about his elbow. Finally, she can't take it any longer and she drags him to the doctor. All the way Harry is complaining about how all doctors are con artists and that modern medicine is all a sham.

At the doctor's office the doctor looks him over for two minutes and tells Harry that he has tennis elbow.

"See what I was telling you, all doctors are quacks!" Harry tells his wife.

The doctor says, "Sorry but you do have tennis elbow, but let's do a few more tests to make sure I'm right and I'll see you again tomorrow.

Harry is given a urine jar and told to fill it first thing in the morning then bring it into the office.

Harry really wants to prove that modern medicine is all quackery so he devises a plan to test the doctor's knowledge. He put a little of his wife's pee in the jar and a little bit of his daughter's pee. He even puts a little bit of his dog's pee in the jar. And for good measure he puts a sperm sample in there too.

When Harry and his wife meet with the doctor, the doctor looks over the test results and states, "Your wife has gonorrhea, your daughter is pregnant, and your dog has a urinary tract infection. And, if you don't stop jerking off, you'll never get rid of your tennis elbow."

I tell this joke to physician groups and find that they really like it. It tends to lead to "patients from hell" stories which are always fun... as long as they are not your patients.

327. ☆☆☆☆☆☆☆☆☆

When Patrick O'Brian was getting ready to leave Ireland he made a pact with his two older brothers. Every day after work each of them would have a stiff drink and toast each other's health.

So everyday Patty went to a bar and ordered three shots of whisky." One for me and one for each of my older brothers back home in Ireland." And every day he toasted his brothers.

Then, one day he came into his favorite pub and ordered his regular and an empty water glass. He took the three shots and poured them into the larger glass.

"Oh, Patty my boy," the barkeep said. "Something happen to your beloved brothers, they didn't die did they?"

"Ah no," Patty said, "It's worse than that——they joined AA."

328. ☆ ☆ ☆ ☆ ☆ ☆ ☆ ☆ ☆

Sarah and Crystal met at their kids' school and became friends. One day while waiting to pick up the kids Crystal said, "Sarah what did you do last night?"

"Well it was a normal night. After the kids were asleep Herby patted the couch and asked me to sit with him. He put his hand on my thigh and I put my hand on his thigh. Then we sang Jewish songs for a few hours."

"That's sounds nice," said Crystal.

"Crystal, what did you do last night." asked Sarah.

"Kind of the same. Tony came home late, the kids were already asleep. He sat on the couch and patted the cushion next to him. So I sat down. He put his hand on my thigh and I put a hand on his thigh then he ravaged me like a crazed stallion for hours."

"Oy, that sounds nice," said Sarah as she fanned herself.

"We do that a lot," said Crystal. "We don't know any Jewish songs."

329. ☆ ☆ ☆ ☆ ☆ ☆ ☆ ☆ ☆

The marriage counselor asked the couple, "You folks don't seem to have anything in common, why on earth did you two get married?"

"I guess it's the old story of opposites attract," the wife said. "He wasn't pregnant and I was."

330. ☆ ☆ ☆ ☆ ☆ ☆ ☆ ☆ ☆

Mr. Worthington and his wife were playing golf. On the 7th hole, Mr. Worthington sliced the ball and it went right into the gardener's shack.

His wife offered to hold the door open so he could play on. Mr. Worthington was intrigued with the challenge and he planned his approach accordingly. Unfortunately, he accidentally hit his wife in the temple with the ball and she died.

Years later, Mr. Worthington was again on the 7th hole and again sliced the ball into the gardener's shack. His partner offered to hold the door for him so he could play on.

"Oh no," Worthington said. "I tried that once and it took me seven shots to get out!"

331. ☆ ☆ ☆ ☆ ☆ ☆ ☆ ☆ ☆ ☆

There was this old man sitting on his front porch rocking his life away when he saw a kid coming down the street carrying a beat up piece of chicken wire.

"Hey kid, what you doing there?" the old man asked.

"I'm going to catch me some chickens," said the kid.

"Ya damn fool, you can't catch no chicken with chicken wire!" growled the old coot.

That evening the same kid came walking back with six chickens entwined in the chicken wire.

The next day the kid comes strolling by holding a long piece of duct tape.

"Hey kid, what you doing there?" grumped the old man.

"I'm going to catch me some ducks," said the kid.

"Ya damn fool, you can't catch no ducks with duct tape!"

That evening the kid comes walking back dragging 5 ducks all entangled in duct tape.

The next morning the kid comes walking by holding a bouquet of pussy willows. The old man sees this and smiles, "Hold on sonny whilst I get my hat!"

332.   ☆ ☆ ☆ ☆ ☆ ☆ ☆ ☆ ☆

The Vatican was having trouble with a very old church bell. They got in the bell repair people who decided that because of the age and importance of the bell, it would be best if Herschel the Bell Maker from Tel Aviv, Israel be brought in to do the job.

Herschel flew to Rome to look at the bell. It was delicate work but the bell was successfully repaired. The next Sunday over 100,000 people came to hear the bell ring in the sunset service.

Right on time and in perfect pitch the bell pealed, "goyyyyyy-immmm, goyyyyyy-immmm, goyyyyyy-immmm..."

333.   ☆ ☆ ☆ ☆ ☆ ☆ ☆ ☆ ☆

The zookeeper takes the gorilla to play golf. At the first tee the zookeeper explains to the gorilla that the goal is to get the ball as close as possible to the green area of grass way over there. The gorilla, holding the golf club in one hand, whacks the ball. The ball sails all the way to the green. The zookeeper is amazed.

The zookeeper takes three strokes to get to the green. Once

there, the zookeeper explains to the gorilla that the goal is to get the ball into the tiny little cup with the flag stuck in it.

The gorilla looks pissed and says, "Damn it Harvey, why didn't you tell me that way back there?"

334. ☆ ☆ ☆ ☆ ☆ ☆ ☆ ☆ ☆ ☆

Patrick Murray said, "God created alcohol just to stop the Irish from ruling the world."

335. ☆ ☆ ☆ ☆ ☆ ☆ ☆ ☆ ☆ ☆

Mr. and Mrs. Goldberg were all excited for their son's upcoming bar mitzvah. Mr. Goldberg told the bar mitzvah coordinator, "This has to be the best bar mitzvah ever, money is no object."

"I just want to warn you Mr. Goldberg," the coordinator said, "bar mitzvah parties can be very expensive."

"I don't care!" barked Mr. Goldberg. "Last year my business

partner had a great bash for his son. For months that's all anybody talked about. He rented Madison Square Garden and had the Harlem Globetrotters play basketball with all the children from the Temple. Afterwards, my partner, that schmuck, flew in Chinese food directly from China. It was served by the Peking Acrobats. What a show off. Not that it matters, but my son's bar mitzvah has to be bigger! Bigger and better I say!"

"OK, Mr. Goldberg," said the coordinator, "I can put together the best bar mitzvah party in the history of bar mitzvah parties."

After months of preparation the important day arrived. The bar mitzvah coordinator had everything going in military fashion.

As soon as the service was over, the group of 200 was helicoptered from New York to Bruce Springstein's mansion in New Jersey. There they were wined and dined and the bar mitzvah boy got to cut a single with his favorite musician, Bruce Springstein.

After dessert, none other than Oprah Winfrey came out to tell about the next part of the party. "I'm taking you all to Africa for your very own bar mitzvah SAFARI!"

The helicopters took all to JFK, and a private Boeing 767 whisked them off to Kenya.

After a good night's sleep on the plane, the 200 honored guests were given full safari gear and photographers from Nation Geographic met with each guest to teach them how to use their new camera equipment.

After rides in Land Rovers got the bar mitzvah party deep into the jungle, elephants awaited to take them all to enjoy the lion photo shoot.

The Prime Minister of Kenya, Raila Odinga himself, sat with the bar mitzvah boy and his proud parents upon the gold covered lead elephant.

After waiting for about 20 minutes, the Prime Minister yelled down to the coordinator, "What is the delay?"

"I'm sorry Mr. Odinga," the coordinator said sheepishly. "It seems that we have to wait for the bar mitzvah safari ahead of us to move off the trail."

336.   ☆ ☆ ☆ ☆ ☆ ☆ ☆ ☆

Mr. Moskowitz was in the bedroom enjoying a little husband

and wife time, if you know what I mean, with his wife. When he looked over and saw the dog yawn a giant yawn. So he said to the dog, "I'm sorry I'm boring you."

"It's alright," the wife said, "I'm used to it."

337. ☆ ☆ ☆ ☆ ☆ ☆ ☆ ☆ ☆ ☆

Old friends are sitting in the living-room waiting for dinner.

"My doctor has me on this new diet to help me with my Alzheimer's," Albert tells his friend.

"Is it helping?"

"Yeah, it's amazing, I'm remembering things like I was twenty again."

"That's great, who's your doctor?"

"You know that plant. Ah... It has thorns and is red..."

"You talking about a rose?"

"Yeah. Hey Rose," Albert yells into the kitchen, "what's my doctor's name?"

338. ☆ ☆ ☆ ☆ ☆ ☆ ☆ ☆ ☆ ☆

When reaching for the potatoes Father Timothy accidentally brushed his arm against Sister Mary Margaret's breast. He was embarrassed and apologized profusely.

"That's OK Father Timothy," Sister Mary said. "As long as you don't get into the habit."

339. ☆ ☆ ☆ ☆ ☆ ☆ ☆ ☆ ☆ ☆

"Half of all people are below average," the psychologist tells the lecture hall. "But with years of clinical experience, I have come to the conclusion that this number is probably low."

340. ☆ ☆ ☆ ☆ ☆ ☆ ☆ ☆

Mr. Levy had made a lot of money in the import-export business. So, he pulled his team of buyers together and told them he wanted to buy the perfect present for his mother's 80th birthday. The team looked high and low for the best present for their boss' mother.

Following the team's recommendation, Mr. Levy procured a rare African Gray parrot that was schooled in five languages, one of them Yiddish, his mother's native tongue.

Mr. Levy had the parrot delivered to his mother in a gilded cage along with some of her favorite chocolates and a large bouquet of flowers.

"Ma, did you like my gift? It is very rare and extremely expensive," Mr. Levy said when he called.

"How expensive can an old chicken be, but I did like the cage, you're such a good son."

"What do you mean old chicken?" Mr. Levy asked.

"At first I thought it would be stringy, but I was wrong. After I boiled it up it turned out to be lovely."

"You ate the parrot?"

"What parrot? I cooked up an old gray chicken, but it was delicious, you're such a good son."

"Ma," Mr. Levy explained, That was no chicken! That was a $5000 African Gray that could communicate in five languages, even Yiddish!"

"So?" his mother asked. "If he was all that smart, when I put a big pot to boil on the stove, why didn't he say something?"

341. ☆ ☆ ☆ ☆ ☆ ☆ ☆ ☆

For her 85th birthday Rubin hired a limo and took his mother to see "Fiddler on the Roof." After the performance Rubin said to his mom, "Ma, what did you think of the play?"

"It was marvelous," the birthday girl said. "It brought back memories of my village in the old country. The memories of family and of course the horrors of the time. But, to tell you the truth, I don't remember so much singing."

342. ☆ ☆ ☆ ☆ ☆ ☆ ☆ ☆ ☆

Jake the bartender is watching over an empty bar when a humungous gorilla trudges in and comes up to the bar. "Beer," the gorilla grunts as he waves a ten dollar bill at Jake.

Jake can't see any reason not to serve a gorilla so he pours the great ape a glass and takes the ten dollars.

The gorilla goes to a nearby table and sits down. Jake, not knowing if a gorilla can count, decides to test the primate.

Jake goes over to the gorilla and hands him a dollar change and says, "Don't get a lot of gorillas in here."

The gorilla sips his beer and says, "Not surprising at nine bucks a beer."

343. ☆ ☆ ☆ ☆ ☆ ☆ ☆ ☆ ☆

Mr. Braverman and Mr. Moskowitz leave their offices at about the same time everyday and meet at the elevator. Every Friday, as they step off the elevator to go their separate ways, they say to each other, "good Shabbos[3]."

Finally one Friday, Mr. Braverman asks, "Every week you say to me 'good Shabbos,' but I don't know you very well, what does a good Shabbos mean to you?"

"Well," Mr. Moskowitz says, "I go home, have a nice dinner with the family, maybe sing some songs. Saturday I go to the synagogue and pray and visit with friends. In the afternoon, I like to nap. Then around 4, I go back to synagogue and pray and visit. Saturday night we tend to have people over for dinner. It's very relaxing. What does Shabbos mean for you?

"After work I pick up my 27 year old shiksa[4] wife," Mr. Braverman explains, "and we drive to our cottage at the shore. Now that the kids are grown, my wife and I lounge around and have a lot of sex. We also eat and walk on the beach. Late Sunday night we come back to the city. I call that a good Shabbos."

---

[3] The jewish weekly day of rest.

[4] A disparaging term for a non-Jewish girl or woman.

"Oy," says Braverman, "That's a <u>great</u> Shabbos!"

344. ☆ ☆ ☆ ☆ ☆ ☆ ☆ ☆ ☆

Mr. Cohen took the first vacation of his life. For 45 years he scrimped and saved while working in the garment district, now finally a well deserved cruise on a luxury ocean liner.

On the 6th day of the cruise, disaster happened and all were lost except Mr. Cohen who washed up on an uninhabited island, with nary a scratch on him. After a few weeks of waiting to be rescued, Mr. Cohen decided that he needed to stay busy before he lost his mind. So, he set out to build himself a lovely hut. He used his sewing skills to make a very nice home. As the years went by, Mr. Cohen kept building until he had built a whole town. He designed a movie house, a general store, and even a temple to worship in.

After 6 years, his town was noticed by a passing plane and a rescue ship was sent.

The captain himself came on the dingy to see what was going on. When the captain found only Mr. Cohen he was intrigued.

"You built all this yourself?" the captain asked.

"Sure, as my mother would say, idle hands…" Mr. Cohen said.

"It is magnificent, the detail, the authenticity… I am very impressed," said the captain. "But, I don't understand. Why do you have two houses of worship?"

"Well," said Mr. Cohen while getting agitated, "this is my synagogue and that one over there… I wouldn't go to even if you paid me!"

345. ☆ ☆ ☆ ☆ ☆ ☆ ☆ ☆ ☆

"Did you ever notice the couple across the street?" Sophie asked her husband. "When he gets home she gives him a hug and he gives her a gentle kiss on the cheek. Why don't you do that?"

"I guess you're right, I need to get to know her."

346. ☆ ☆ ☆ ☆ ☆ ☆ ☆ ☆ ☆

Two nice Jewish old ladies are talking at the retirement home.

"Hilda, do you still get, you know, horny?"

"Yeah I sure do, sometimes," Hilda says.

"What do you do when you get horny?"

"I suck a lifesaver," Hilda says, "until the feeling passes."

"That's a good idea," Sarah says, "But who drives you to the beach?"

"This is highly inappropriate... But, yes... unfortunately he did swallow a quarter."

347. ☆ ☆ ☆ ☆ ☆ ☆ ☆ ☆ ☆

A young rabbi comes up to a table of women at the synagogue's annual picnic and says, "Good afternoon ladies, is anything alright?"

348. ☆ ☆ ☆ ☆ ☆ ☆ ☆ ☆ ☆

Christians are lucky, they get to confess. Every Sunday they can tell their mistakes and get absolution. Jews don't get to confess in the same way. Rabbis don't understand like priests do.

Mr. Greenberg goes to the older rabbi and says, "Rabbi I need to tell you, I had an affair."

"That's nice Mr. Greenberg," said the rabbi, "Who catered it?

Was there a band?"

349. ☆ ☆ ☆ ☆ ☆ ☆ ☆ ☆ ☆

Over the years, boy have I heard this joke a lot in my office:

Why do divorces cost so much?
Because they're worth it!

350. ☆ ☆ ☆ ☆ ☆ ☆ ☆ ☆ ☆

Mr. Schlemiel goes to the doctor's office with a severe stutter. After a thorough examination the doctor explains.

"Your stuttering is due to the enormity of your penis. It's pulling on your diaphragm causing you to stutter."

"C-c-c-can y-y-you h-h-h-help m-m-m-me?" Mr. Schlemiel asks.

"Sure, with a relatively simple surgery we can remove your massive penis and replace it with a normal sized penis. That should solve the problem," the doctor explains.

Mr. Schlemiel wants the operation.

Six months later Mr. Schlemiel comes into the doctor's office and says, "My sex life is awful, I'd rather stutter… can you reverse the operation?"

The doctor puts a consoling hand on Mr. Schlemiel's shoulder and says, "N-n-n no."

351. ☆ ☆ ☆ ☆ ☆ ☆ ☆ ☆ ☆

Old Mr. Leibovitz was awakened by a terrible earthquake. He sat up and rubbed sleep out of his eyes. He looked around the room and saw his wife sleeping comfortably. Then he noticed the sounds of chains and moans of pain. The sounds got louder and the room started to glow red. The smell of death hovered in the air. As the room got hotter, flames erupted in all directions. Appearing out of the heat and smoke the Prince of Darkness glared at Mr. Leibovitz.

"I am Lucifer, lord of the underworld," the Devil shrieked. "Bow down before me! Fear me!"

"No thank you," Mr. Leibovitz said.

"Aren't you afraid of me!" The Devil screamed. "I am Satan, Beelzebub, the Evil One!"

"Why would I be afraid of you?" Mr. Leibovitz said as he patted his wife on her rump. "I've been married to your mother-in-law for 42 years."

352. ☆ ☆ ☆ ☆ ☆ ☆ ☆ ☆ ☆ ☆

My Aunt Sadie went with two girlfriends to a fancy hotel in the Caribbean. When she got back I asked her about the trip.

"It was very nice if you like that sort of thing," Sadie said. "The first day we went to the nice sand beach and put down some towels. It was different. It was a nudest beach. After a minute a man came over to collect his Frisbee and stood right there in front of us with his schmuck[5] dangling right there. Eva had a stroke. I was petrified. Then Becky had a stroke..."

"Oh my god," I said, "what did you do?"

"Me? Nothing! I wouldn't touch that thing!"

353. ☆ ☆ ☆ ☆ ☆ ☆ ☆ ☆ ☆

A rabbi, a priest and a minister were talking about how difficult the economy was on collections. As they talked the question of how much each personally made from their chosen profession came up.

The priest said, I have a simple way. Whatever comes in the collection plate, I get 10%.

The three men nodded with agreement.

Then the minister said, "I get about 12 to 14 percent. I pray for God to provide while I take my hat and place it on the floor. Then I throw all the money high into the air, what God lets fall into the hat is mine."

"I too have a hat," said the rabbi. "I also put it on the floor. I also throw all the money high into the air as I pray for God's direction. I pray loudly to the heavens, 'Here is your money, do with it what you may.'"

"I figure," the rabbi continued, "What God wants—he keeps. What falls back to the ground—is mine."

354. ☆ ☆ ☆ ☆ ☆ ☆ ☆ ☆ ☆

Markowitz, the world renowned clothing designer, was putting on a dinner for his wife's 50th birthday. Money was no object. Only the best of everything.

Early on in the evening, the head housekeeper comes and tells him that there was no toilet paper to be found anywhere in the mansion.

Thinking fast, Markowitz has the waitstaff cut up hundreds of dress patterns that he had stored away in the basement. "Doily sized squares," he orders.

The party was a great success. As three ladies were waiting for the valet to bring their car, the first lady said, "This was the nicest

---

[5] Yiddish for penis.

party I have ever been to. The harpist in the foyer set a wonderful tone for the whole evening."

The second lady said, "The cuisine was grand. King crab and those little puff pastries. Excellent, simply exquisite."

The third lady said, "I was really impressed with the bathroom. It had the fanciest toilet paper I have ever seen."

"Toilet paper?" the ladies asked.

"Yes, It was really classy. I've never seen it marked 'front' and 'back' before."

355.   ☆ ☆ ☆ ☆ ☆ ☆ ☆ ☆ ☆

The golf pro was a complete wreck when he called his psychologist to make an emergency appointment.

"Thanks for seeing me today, Doc," the golf pro said. "I've been a bundle of nerves since I lost to old Rabbi Horowitz today."

"Rabbi Horowitz, isn't he in his eighties?"

"He just turned 94," said the pro. "I played a round of golf with him this morning, and lost!"

"How did that happen, did you give him too large of a handicap?" asked the psychologist.

"No, that's part of the problem. I offered the rabbi a handicap before we started, and he politely told me he didn't need any strokes, just two gotchas."

"Two gotchas?" asked the therapist.

"I didn't know what the old man was taking about either, but I figured I could let him have some fun playing a round of golf with me then I could call it a day. Well, I went up to the first tee and just as I was swinging to hit the ball, that old geezer ran up behind me and reached through my legs, grabbed my testicles with his bony hand and yelled 'gotcha'"!

"Wow, that's unbelievable," said the shrink. "But that was only one stroke so I don't see how you could possibly lose."

"That's the point, doc," said the pro. "Do you know how hard it is to play golf waiting for that second gotcha?"

356. ☆ ☆ ☆ ☆ ☆ ☆ ☆ ☆ ☆

"I think you have the wrong number," Harold said to the caller. "I'm sorry, you will have to call the weather bureau for that information."

"Who was that Harold?" Sylvia asked.

"I don't know," said Harold, "some fool wanting to know if the coast was clear."

357. ☆ ☆ ☆ ☆ ☆ ☆ ☆ ☆ ☆

Two old friends were kvetching[6] with my uncle Morty about being old.

"I hate it, I can't even pee," Aaron says. "My prostrate's the size of a beach ball. I push and I push and, if I'm lucky, I get a few drops.

"I hear you," says Marvin. "My bowels have become the enemy. I push and I strain and I'm lucky if I can get raisins. Raisins I tell you!"

"I understand, getting old isn't for sissies," Uncle Morty says. "In the morning at 8 AM I enjoy a nice pee. A wonderful stream. I'm like a fountain. Then, I have a nice bowel movement. It's like passing plums, I tell you. Nice juicy plums."

"That sounds wonderful," says Aaron.

"You would think so," nodded Uncle Morty, "but I don't get up

---

[6] Yiddish meaning to complain.

until nine, sometimes nine fifteen."

358. ☆ ☆ ☆ ☆ ☆ ☆ ☆ ☆ ☆

A Scotsman goes into a bar after the parade. After blowing on his bagpipes for hours he needed a few stiff ones. He drank one after another then needs to go pee. He stands up and gets lightheaded. He falls straight backwards and passes out.

Two ladies see the whole thing and one says to the other, "I always wondered what they wear under their kilts." So they go and peek and find that he's not wearing anything under it.

"Well, that is the most impressive manhood I have ever seen," the first lady says.

"It's a beauty," agrees the second. Then with a giggle she pulls a ribbon out of her hair and ties a big bow on it.

In a little bit, the Scotsman wakes up and realizes he still needs to pee and heads for the men's room.

Standing at the urinal he notices the blue ribbon and says, "I don't know where you've been, but I'm sure proud of you for getting first place!"

359. ☆ ☆ ☆ ☆ ☆ ☆ ☆ ☆ ☆

Old Mr. Rubin was listening to the young men at the club tell their stories of sexual conquests. When the group looked at him for his two-cents he said, "Mrs. Rubin is quite frigid. When she opens her mouth, a little light comes on."

"Not that I'm complaining, sometimes I use that little light to find my way to the bathroom. The other night, I was standing in the bathroom waiting to go, and I realized the floor was cold. OY, with my prostate, I do a lot of standing around in the bathroom. I got upset and I said to Mr. Putz, 'You brought me here now do something.'"

"Mrs. Rubin heard me talking in the bathroom and called out, "who you talking to?"

"No one you'd remember!"

360. ☆ ☆ ☆ ☆ ☆ ☆ ☆ ☆ ☆

Let me tell you another story about Rubin:

Many years after the above last occurred, the Rubins ended up in court petitioning to get a divorce.

The judge looked at the frail elderly couple and said, "I don't mean to be insensitive, but aren't you both a little old for getting a divorce?"

"Well your honor," Mr. Rubin said, "it has been inevitable for many years."

The judge scratched his head and asked, "How old are you two?"

"Your holiness," Mrs. Rubin said, "come May I will be 92 and Mr. Rubin will be 94… God willing."

"We have been married for 75 years," added Mr. Rubin.

"So why are you getting a divorce now?" asked the judge.

"We both thought," nodded Mr. Rubin, "it would be best if we waited for the children to pass."

361. ☆ ☆ ☆ ☆ ☆ ☆ ☆ ☆ ☆

My girlfriend loves cats. I don't understand that. Cats are ornery and messy. They come back at all hours of the night and demand attention. They don't do what you tell them, and they pretend they don't understand the simplest of directions. I don't get it. Everything women love about cats, they hate about men.

362. ☆ ☆ ☆ ☆ ☆ ☆ ☆ ☆ ☆

At the fancy Golf and Tennis Club, Mr. Greenbaum rushes into the men's room. Just in time, he gets into the stall when he hears a slight tap on the wall.

"I envy you," said the voice, "At my age, I've been here for fifteen minutes and nothing! You just come in, and like that, boom boom boom, you're right down to business."

"There's no need to envy me," said Greenbaum. "At my age, I have trouble getting my pants off."

363. ☆ ☆ ☆ ☆ ☆ ☆ ☆ ☆ ☆

Mr. Rubin Moskowitz spent 52 years waiting tables at the Ritz. The day he retired, he got hit by a crosstown bus on its way to the Bronx.

Mrs. Moskowitz was beside herself. For months she cried and kvetched[7]. One night when she was trying to distract herself with some late night TV, an advertisement for a mystic caught her attention.

Mrs. Moskowitz decided to hold a seance so she could say goodbye to her beloved husband.

The medium conducted the seance in a cramped room with dim light and thick incense. With a few of her friends, Mrs. Moskowitz held hands and repeated the chant as instructed. At first nothing. But then the room got darker and the incense got thicker. From a dot of light moving by the ceiling, the figure of a man slowly emerged. The figure got larger and larger.

"Rubin, is that you?" Mrs. Moskowitz asked softly.

The ghostly figure of Mr. Moskowitz bowed its head.

"Rubin, come here," spoke Mrs. Moskowitz. "I need to talk to you."

"I can't," Mr. Moskowitz said with his thick Yiddish accent, "it's not my table."

364. ☆ ☆ ☆ ☆ ☆ ☆ ☆ ☆ ☆

Ms. Cole was concerned about one of her 10 year old students. So she decided to talk to him privately.

"Georgie, I'm worried that your grades are slipping, any idea why?"

"Yes, Ms. Cole," Georgie said as he played nervously with his hands. "I'm in love."

"That's normal for a young man your age Georgie. Who are you in love with?" Ms. Cole said gently.

"With you Ms. Cole."

"Oh... that's very sweet, Georgie... and someday I hope to have my very own husband, but not a child. Do you understand Georgie?

"Yes Ms. Cole," said Georgie, "I'll use a condom."

---

[7] Yiddish for complained a lot.

365. ☆ ☆ ☆ ☆ ☆ ☆ ☆ ☆ ☆

It was a dark night at sea and the fog was as thick as pea soup. The admiral was on board the destroyer preparing for war games off the coast of California.

The admiral was not happy when he saw a dim light dead ahead. He ordered the message be sent, "Veer off."

The admiral was furious when the dim light returned the message, "You veer off."

The admiral took the mic, "This is Admiral Hawthorn, commander of these war games, I order you to veer off or I will…!"

The bright light ahead interrupted, "This is the night janitor of this here lighthouse…"

366. ☆ ☆ ☆ ☆ ☆ ☆ ☆ ☆ ☆

Farmer Brown was at the general store complaining to a friend that his rooster was not performing. His friend offered to lend him his prized rooster, but warned him that he was a crazed sex maniac and he needed to be kept locked in the chicken coup… or else.

Thinking that his friend was pulling his leg, old farmer Brown didn't heed the warning. As soon as the rooster was set loose in the chicken coop, the feathers went a-flying. Squawking and screaming the chickens were serviced over and over by the rooster.

When farmer Brown went to make sure the hens were OK, the rooster ran by him and went after a flock of ducks. The rooster wasn't discriminatory, hen ducks and drakes alike got the once over. After that, the rooster moved onto the goats, then the pigs, and at nightfall the cows were attacked.

All night long the rooster was sowing his seed. The ruckus was nonstop. Deer, horses, tractors—nothing was safe. In the morning, farmer Brown looked out the window and saw the rooster lying motionless in the driveway.

"Oh no," he thought to himself, "I went and killed the rooster because of my neglect."

Farmer Brown ran out of the house towards the worn out rooster. As the farmer knelt next him he opened one eye, pointed skyward with his wing and whispered, "buzzards!"

367. ☆ ☆ ☆ ☆ ☆ ☆ ☆ ☆ ☆

Mrs. Ginsberg was 83 years young. Her children were sending her and Mr. Ginsberg on a world cruise to celebrate their 50th wedding anniversary. Using the cruise as a ruse, the children talked their mother into getting a full physical and even a trip to a gynecologist, something she had never done before.

In the middle of the gynecological examination, Mrs. Ginsberg sat up and tapped the young doctor on the top on his head, "Young man, does your mother know what you do for a living?"

"I think; Therefore, I am single."

368. ☆ ☆ ☆ ☆ ☆ ☆ ☆ ☆ ☆

Jet Blue tried a promotion to increase family travel. For one month they allowed wives to fly free with a full priced purchase of a roundtrip, first class ticket.

Hoping to get some positive endorsements, the airline's promotions department sent questionnaires out asking wives if they liked their free flight on Jet Blue.

To date they have received 1,786 returned questionnaires all saying the same thing: What free flight?

369. ☆ ☆ ☆ ☆ ☆ ☆ ☆ ☆ ☆

Uncle Bernie is visiting Israel with a group of fellow seniors. They spend a week seeing all the holy places by bus. At one of the numerous historical digs, Uncle Bernie takes a wrong turn and finds himself lost. He sits down figuring that someone will come along and help him find his way back to the bus. While sitting there he notices a little shinny something in the sand. He picks it up and realizes it's a tiny old prayer book. He opens the silver clasp and to his surprise an old rabbi pops out. It's a rabbi genie.

"OY," the old rabbi genie says, "Boy is my back sore. I've been stuck in that book for 2000 years. About time you came along. For letting me out, I'll give you one wish."

"One wish?" said Uncle Bernie. "I thought genies gave three wishes?"

"If we want to, but I don't want to. One or none, you pick," grumps the rabbi genie.

"I'll take one," said Uncle Bernie as he takes out a map of the Middle East. "You see this map. I want all the lands on this map to live in peace. Peace is what I want with my wish."

The rabbi genie rubs his long beard and says, "It can't be done. I'm only a genie, I can't help you. Pick something else, I'm in a hurry."

"OK," says Uncle Bernie, "My wife is a nice Jewish woman. She says that nice Jewish women never give oral sex. I want my wife to give me oral sex. That's what I want."

The rabbi genie scratches his head. Ponders his ponder and shakes his head. "Oy, do you ask a lot. OK, let me take a look at that map again."

370. ☆ ☆ ☆ ☆ ☆ ☆ ☆ ☆ ☆

Sister Mary Jacobs comes into Mother Superior's office and delivers the bad news in a whisper. "We have discovered a case of syphilis in the convent."

"How wonderful," Mother Superior clapps happily, "I am so tired of the Chablis."

371. ☆ ☆ ☆ ☆ ☆ ☆ ☆ ☆ ☆

Sister Mary Jacobs was running a little late for early morning prayer when she ran into Sister Margaret. "Good morning Sister Mary Jacobs, I see you got out of the wrong side of the bed this morning."

"No, no just in a hurry," Sister Mary Jacobs said as she continued on.

Getting in line for chapel, Sister Sarah said, "Oh Sister Mary Jacobs, I see you got out of the wrong side of the bed this morning."

"What?"

"I see you got out of the wrong side of the bed this morning."

"Why do people keep saying that to me?" Sister Mary Jacobs asked.

"Because!" The Mother Superior said sternly as she walked by, "You're wearing Father O'Henry's slippers!"

372. ☆ ☆ ☆ ☆ ☆ ☆ ☆ ☆ ☆

Reverend Leroy preached loud and to the point. "Today I want to talk to all you women out there, you will know who you are. All you women who sowed your wild oats last night. That's right, all you women that sowed wild oats last night, then came to church this morning and prayed to the All Mighty for a crop failure. Can I have an Amen?

373. ☆ ☆ ☆ ☆ ☆ ☆ ☆ ☆ ☆

Morty ran into his lawyer's office and said, "What's the penalty for bigamy?"

The lawyer thought for a moment, checked his computer and said, "Two mother-in-laws."

374. ☆ ☆ ☆ ☆ ☆ ☆ ☆ ☆ ☆

Bob and Mary were making small talk during their first date.

"My father taught me how to swim by throwing me out of a rowboat so I had to learn to swim to shore. Then he took me further out into the lake and threw me overboard. But I learned to swim to shore."

"It sounds like your father taught you how to swim the hard way," Mary said.

"Not really, the hard part was getting out of the burlap sack."

375. ☆ ☆ ☆ ☆ ☆ ☆ ☆ ☆ ☆

How many husbands does it take to replace a toilet paper roll?
Who knows, it's never been done!

376. ☆ ☆ ☆ ☆ ☆ ☆ ☆ ☆ ☆

Old Mr. Farnsberg was concerned that his wife was going deaf. So, he walked up behind her and said, "Can you hear me?" No reply.

So he said it a little louder, "Can you hear me?" No reply.

So he said it right into her ear, "Honey, can you hear me?"

"Yes Harold," she yelled, "for the third time I can hear you!"

377. ☆ ☆ ☆ ☆ ☆ ☆ ☆ ☆ ☆

Mrs. Goldfarb couldn't contain her joy.

"My son, Harold, is going to a psychiatrist," she told her best friend.

"Is that good?"

"Good, it's great," gushed Mrs. Goldfarb. "He's spending $300 an hour just to talk about me!"

378. ☆ ☆ ☆ ☆ ☆ ☆ ☆ ☆ ☆

Mr. Rothstein bought a new car. It was a spectacular car and he wanted to get it blessed. He didn't know the religion of the car so he went to the major houses of worship in his neighborhood and offered a donation in exchange for a blessing over his car.

The priest sprinkled holy water and said a prayer in Latin. The minister said a few words and led a silent prayer for the attendees. The rabbi sang from the book of Solomon and cut off the end of the tailpipe.

379. ☆ ☆ ☆ ☆ ☆ ☆ ☆ ☆ ☆

A sudden sound of keys opening the apartment door startled the romantic couple.

"Hurry, it's my husband," said the wife. "Jump out of the window."

"I can't jump out of the window, we're on the 13th floor!" whispered the lover.

"Jump all ready," yelled the wife. "This is no time to be superstitious!"

380. ☆ ☆ ☆ ☆ ☆ ☆ ☆ ☆ ☆

When I was about 8 or 9 I was on Fifth Avenue with my Aunt Sadie. A man in front of us grabbed his chest and fell to the sidewalk. A cop saw what happened and came over to help. The cop called for an ambulance. The paramedics worked to save the man's life. From the back of the crowd my Aunt Sadie yelled out, "Give him some chicken soup."

The paramedics zapped the poor soul with the paddles, and my Aunt Sadie yelled out again, "Give him some chicken soup."

Finally, the paramedics plunge a large syringe of adrenaline into the man's chest as a last ditch effort to save his life. My Aunt Sadie yelled out yet again, "Give him some chicken soup."

As the paramedics pulled a sheet over the poor man's face, once more Aunt Sadie yelled, "Give him some chicken soup."

The parametric looked sadly at my Aunt and said, "I'm sorry lady we have tried everything."

"Give him some chicken soup."

But lady, he is gone. What would chicken soup do for him now?"

"It couldn't hurt!"

381. ☆ ☆ ☆ ☆ ☆ ☆ ☆ ☆ ☆

Two lovers are bumping uglies one afternoon when the woman hears her husband's car pull into the garage.

"Hurry get out, that's my husband."

"Get out?"

"Yeah, now!" she gasps pushing him out the window, "He's a cop and he carries a gun."

The lover goes butt naked out into the rain where he sees a group of joggers running down the street. Figuring it's a good place to hide, he runs into the middle of the pack.

One jogger looks over at him and asks, "Do you always jog nude?"

"Sure," said the lover.

"With a condom on?"

"Only when it rains."

382. ☆ ☆ ☆ ☆ ☆ ☆ ☆ ☆ ☆

Rabbi Morison was recuperating in the hospital after he broke his hip. He received some lovely flowers from his congregation. The note read: "Congregation Beth Israel, by a vote of 311 to 184, wishes you a quick and complete recovery."

383. ☆ ☆ ☆ ☆ ☆ ☆ ☆ ☆ ☆

Mr. Eagleclaw spoke to my Uncle Sol concerning French lined, night black braziers.

"I can get them for you," but they're a little pricy. What sizes do you want?"

"I can only use size 38 Double D. How much for say, 50?"

"For you, Mr. Eagleclaw, $50 each."

A week later, Mr. Eagleclaw ordered 50 more, and just 3 days later he ordered 100 more.

Uncle Sol was wondering what was going on so he placed a call.

"Mr. Eagleclaw," Uncle Sol said. "Thank you so much for your business, but I'm curious, what do you do with so many French lined, night black, 38 double D, braziers?

"Oh," Mr. Eagleclaw said, "I cut them in half and sell each cup as lucky yarmulkes to rich Jews that come to my casino."

384. ☆ ☆ ☆ ☆ ☆ ☆ ☆ ☆ ☆

My friend Jimmy Eagleclaw told me that his father doesn't like being call "Indian" or "Native America" anymore. He wants to be called a 'Casino Owning American' from now on.

385. ☆ ☆ ☆ ☆ ☆ ☆ ☆ ☆ ☆

Bob is really drunk and he gets it into his head that he wants to go ice fishing. So he gets his gear and goes out onto the ice. Just as he gets ready to hack a hole in the ice with his axe he hears a booming voice, "There's no fish under the ice!"

"What?" Bob says to the heavens, "God, is that you?"

"No," thunders the great voice, "It's me, Harold, the ice rink manager!"

386. ☆ ☆ ☆ ☆ ☆ ☆ ☆ ☆ ☆

When it is my time to die, I want to go like my grandfather, peacefully in my sleep. Not screaming and petrified like the passengers in his car.

387. ☆ ☆ ☆ ☆ ☆ ☆ ☆ ☆ ☆

Mrs. Burkowitz was despondent after her husband's death. After 63 years of marriage she couldn't see going on. She wanted to be in heaven with her beloved.

As she pondered her options she was sure that she wanted to go quickly. And she was doubly sure that she didn't want to botch it and take a chance of being a burden on her two wonderful boys or her perfect grandchildren.

After great thought, she decided to use Mr. Burkowitz's old army revolver and shoot herself in the heart. There was one problem. She wasn't exactly sure where her heart was. So she called the hospital and a nurse told her it was just below her left breast.

That evening, Mrs. Burkowitz was taken to the hospital with a bullet hole in her left knee.

388. ☆ ☆ ☆ ☆ ☆ ☆ ☆ ☆ ☆ ☆

Little Stanley busted into tears right after he turned on the lights in his parents' bedroom. After 30 minutes of consoling him, Stanley was finally able to get his thoughts out.

"Mommy, you yell at me for just sucking my own thumb!"

389. ☆ ☆ ☆ ☆ ☆ ☆ ☆ ☆ ☆

How many lawyers does it take to shingle a house?
It depends on how thin you slice them.

390. ☆ ☆ ☆ ☆ ☆ ☆ ☆ ☆ ☆

My Uncle Erving was finally getting to go to Miami for a little rest and relaxation. He was a little concerned about traveling from New York City to Miami all alone by train, so he stopped into a nice bar just around the corner from Grand Central Station.

By the time Uncle Erving made it to the train, he was happy go-lucky and singing softly to himself. "I'm going to Miami to get me vacation."

When the conductor came by, Uncle Erving was feeling no pain. "I'm going to Miami to get me vacation."

The conductor asked for Uncle Erving's ticket.

♪"I'm going to Miami to get me vacation."♪

"Hey mister, your ticket, PLEASE!" barked the conductor.

♪"I'm going to Miami to get me vacation."♪

"Hey mister you got a ticket?"

♪"I'm going to Miami to get me vacation."♪ Uncle Erving sang to himself.

"Mister you've got to show me your ticket and get your bag out of the aisle!" The conductor grumped.

♪"I'm going to Miami to get me vacation."♪

Mister if you don't stop singing that, and move your bag right now, I'll throw it out the window!"

♪"I'm going to Miami to get me vacation."♪

The conductor was pissed. He picked up the bag and shoved it out the window.

♪"I'm going to Miami to get me vacation."♪

"What's wrong with you?" yelled the conductor. "Aren't you pissed that I threw your bag out the window?"

♩ ♪ ♫ ♬ ♭ "I'm going to Miami to get me vacation and that wasn't my baa aaa g." ♩ ♪ ♫ ♬ ♭

391. ☆ ☆ ☆ ☆ ☆ ☆ ☆ ☆ ☆ ☆

A teenager, a black man, and a Chicano are driving in a car. Who's driving?

The cop.

"There's no easy way to say this... our angel investor died."

392. ☆ ☆ ☆ ☆ ☆ ☆ ☆ ☆ ☆ ☆

What has 4 legs and an arm?
A very happy pit bull.

393. ☆ ☆ ☆ ☆ ☆ ☆ ☆ ☆ ☆ ☆

What do you call a lawyer buried in sand up to his chin?
Not enough sand.

394. ☆ ☆ ☆ ☆ ☆ ☆ ☆ ☆ ☆

Why did the shark refuse to eat the lawyer?
Professional courtesy.

395. ☆ ☆ ☆ ☆ ☆ ☆ ☆ ☆

Larry was playing golf. It was not a good day for Larry. As he took a break from swearing and throwing his clubs, he spied three elderly Jewish men playing through.

Each man set the ball on the tee, said a prayer over the ball, and proceeded to send the ball sailing onto the green.

Abandoning his gear, Larry followed the men and watched the same great performance hole after hole.

Finally, he worked up the nerve to go talk to these great golfers.

"Excuse me sirs," Larry asked. "How did you learn to play so well?"

The oldest man said, "We don't get out to the golf course too often. Wish we did, but we spend a lot of our time studying the Torah. By studying the holy books, God has blessed our golf game.

Larry pondered this for a few days then decided to dedicate himself to the Torah. He joined a Temple, and he studied scripture night and day. As it turned out he was a good student.

After not touching his golf clubs for over a year, Larry decided to see how his golf game was coming. He went to the country club and at the first tee he found the three old Jewish men teeing off. He told them about his study of Torah, and they invited him to play a round with them.

Larry set the ball and reverently said a blessing over it. He squared his shoulders and relaxed his hips. He kept his eyes on the ball, swung and "whack"! The ball flew off into the tree line.

"I don't get it," Larry cried in frustration. "I studied the holy books, I live a good life!"

The older Jew consoled him, "What Temple have you been studying at?

"I belong to Temple Beth-El," Larry said.

"Oh, I see your problem, Temple Beth-El is for Tennis."

396.   ☆ ☆ ☆ ☆ ☆ ☆ ☆ ☆

Rabbi Fineberg and Father O'Riley have been friends for many years. After a charity event, they find themselves at the hotel bar, one sheet to the wind.

"Rabbi, my good friend, when are you going to let me buy you a fine ham dinner?" Father O'Riley ribbed.

"I'll be happy to let you," Rabbi Fineberg smiled, "at your wedding."

I have not heard this joke much. A more common version follows:

397.   ☆ ☆ ☆ ☆ ☆ ☆ ☆ ☆

Rabbi Fineberg and Father O'Riley are talking about the difficulties of serving God, their chosen professions.

"I don't mean to pry Father," said Rabbi Fineberg, "But have you ever been with a woman?"

"Alas just once," the Father said in a hushed tone, "Before I was ordained."

"Well old friend, so you're the person I can ask," said Rabbi Fineberg. "It's better than ham don't you think?"

398.   ☆ ☆ ☆ ☆ ☆ ☆ ☆ ☆

Mr. Moskowitz was celebrating his 85th birthday. His two sons took him to the Ritz for an amazing meal then put him up in the Presidential Suite for the night.

When he heard a knock at the door, Mr. Moskowitz was surprised, because it was so late. He shuffled off to the door and opened it, and to his surprise there was a lovely lady standing there. She opened her coat to reveal nothing but what God gave her, and she said, "Your sons sent me to you so you can have super sex on your birthday."

"OK," Mr. Moskowitz said, "I'll take the soup."

399. ☆ ☆ ☆ ☆ ☆ ☆ ☆ ☆ ☆

A man and a woman meet at a business conference. Throughout the day they seemed to have a lot in common. Near the end of the first day of meetings the man asked the woman if she would like to have dinner and maybe a little dancing afterwards.

She said, "That would be nice, but I just want to tell you that I have acute angina."

"Well I hope so," said the man, "because your tits are nothing to write home about."

"Now listen up ... As soon as the plane doors close you press play. This blasts the Afghan national anthem throughout the cabin. Arrest anyone who stands up!

400.   ☆☆☆☆☆☆☆☆☆

Vegetarian is Native American for bad hunter.

401.   ☆☆☆☆☆☆☆☆

Herby Ginsberg was sixty-seven when he got married to a baby of twenty-seven. As time went by, Herby and his wife were having trouble conceiving. The doctor told Herby he should check his sperm count.

Herby goes for the test and a nice nurse gives him a specimen jar and tells him to go into the room down the hall and try to relax. She tells him to watch the movies or read the magazines that are there to help him get into the mood to produce a sperm sample.

Herby is a little nervous while hearing this from the nice nurse but he goes into the room.

Many hours later the nurse is a little concerned, so she goes over to knock on the door. To her surprise, she hears what sounds like a bar fight going on in there. She knocks again and says, "Mr. Ginsberg are you alright?"

Herby opened the door a crack. He is covered in sweat and his glasses are hanging from one ear.

"I've tried everything," he gasped. "I pulled on it. I squeezed it and tugged on it. I used my teeth. I even slammed it against the toilet, but I can't get the top off this damn jar."

402. ☆ ☆ ☆ ☆ ☆ ☆ ☆ ☆

Dr. Fineberg is a researcher at NYU. His specialty is human sexuality. He received a huge research grant to study his chosen subject so he decides to find out what really is the best sexual position. He studies the research articles and all the books on the subject, but he is not satisfied that he has truly uncovered the scientific proof. And as you know, inquiring minds want to know.

So, Dr. Fineberg decides to do field research. He goes to the brothels all over New York City and conducts extensive scientific interviews. Very quickly he hears about the old Jewish hooker with one eye. As he investigates further, he finds that most people that know of such matters, agree she is the best at sex in the known universe.

He tracks down the old Jewish lady with one eye, and knocks on her door. "Come in bubelah[8]," an old voice calls.

Dr. Fineberg enters and is not prepared for what he sees. There on the bed is a very old woman. She is thin and wrinkled and wearing a teddy that reveals too much.

"Come on in bubelah," she says. Don't be afraid. I will give you the experience of a lifetime."

Dr. Fineberg hastily tries to explain that he is a researcher…

The old lady simply says, "Stick it in my eye hole it's OK."

Again Dr. Fineberg tries to explain…

"Stick it in my eye hole, you'll be very happy you did," the old lady repeats.

I'm sure you can guess what happens next. Dr. Fineberg does as he is instructed, and he is overwhelmed with pleasure. In his whole

---

[8] Yiddish. Darling, sweetheart - especially a child.

life he has never dreamed of such ecstasy.

As Dr. Fineberg is getting ready to leave, he finds himself praising the old woman.

"I'm going to tell everyone I know about you. You are amazing!" he gasps.

"That's nice bubelah," the old lady says. "I'll keep an eye out for 'em."

403. ☆ ☆ ☆ ☆ ☆ ☆ ☆ ☆ ☆

Larry was out drinking with Marty and was amazed that it had turned 4 AM.

"Marty, if I go home now, no matter how quietly I sneak into the house, my wife will be furious and scream at me for hours. What am I to do?"

"Larry do what I do," Marty said. "I park out front of the house and slam the door of the car as loud as I can. I go in the front door singing old navy songs at the top of my lungs. When I get into the bedroom I strip down and hop into bed with extra bounce making sure I pull the covers off my wife. Then I slap her on the rump and say, 'I love you honey… give me some sugar!"

"Really?" said Larry.

"Sure, and just to spite me she pretends to be asleep!"

404. ☆ ☆ ☆ ☆ ☆ ☆ ☆ ☆ ☆

My Uncle Sol and Uncle Morty were discussing their day. As usual, each wanted to one up the other with their salesmanship story.

"Today I sold an order for 2700 pants to Macy's. I even got a bonus kicked-in for early delivery. This sale alone will keep us in blintzes for many months to come. You know it wouldn't hurt for you to watch when I close a big sale—you could learn a few things," Uncle Morty bragged.

"I also had a good day," smiled Uncle Sol. "I sold a black silk suit to Mrs. Goldfarb for her husband's funeral, may he rest in peace."

"You sold one suit and you think that makes you a better salesman than me!" Uncle Morty laughed.

"I also sold her a second pair of pants."

405. ☆ ☆ ☆ ☆ ☆ ☆ ☆ ☆ ☆

On a US military transport plane filled with soldiers eager to get home and put Afghanistan behind them, a rumor circulated that the flight crew were all women. The young soldiers seemed unfazed, but a few of the older GI's were a little uneasy. One master sergeant asked a passing flight crew member, "Is it true ma'am, that all the personnel in the cockpit are women?"

"Yes master sergeant, it's not a cockpit any more."

406. ☆ ☆ ☆ ☆ ☆ ☆ ☆ ☆ ☆

Aunt Sadie was very worried about Uncle Sol so she went to the doctor.

"My Sol," she said, "I think he is losing, you know, his potency, ah… in the bedroom."

"Well Sol is getting on in years Sadie, this may be normal," consoled the doctor.

"Normal?"

"Yes normal. You and Sol are in your 80's now, things change. When did you first notice Sol's problem?" the doctor asked.

Aunt Sadie wrung her hands with anxiety, "Well, first yesterday afternoon, then twice last night, then again this morning."

407. ☆ ☆ ☆ ☆ ☆ ☆ ☆ ☆ ☆

Soon after Moshe Cohen's business went public he bought an expensive condo in an upscale building on the lower east side. When he first met his neighbor he wanted to make a good impression.

"Nice to meet you, I'm truly looking forward to us becoming vast friends," said Moshe.

"Good afternoon, sir. I'm Reginard Browne of the Connecticut Browne's, spelled B-R-O-W-N-E. I don't wish to be rude, but I do not approve of letting immigrants into this building. For I am white from the tip if my head to the tip of my toes,"

"Oy, I understand," said Moshe, "Immigrants can be annoying. I too am white from the tip of my head to the tip of my toes, except for a little brown spot in the middle of my behind, spelled B-R-O-W-N-E."

408. ☆ ☆ ☆ ☆ ☆ ☆ ☆ ☆ ☆

Harry was out ice fishing but having no luck. Just 20 feet away an old timer was hauling in fish after fish. After the old timer pulled in a huge walleye, Harry had to find out his secret.

"Sorry to interrupt you mister," Harry said, "but do you have a secret or something?"

"Mum mmm mm mmmm mmm mmmmm mmmm," the old codger mumbled.

"What?" said Harry.

"Mum mmm mm mmmm mmm mmmmm mmmm."

"What???"

The old man spit a wad into his hand and said, "You got to keep the worms warm!"

409. ☆ ☆ ☆ ☆ ☆ ☆ ☆ ☆ ☆

Mr. and Mrs. Horowitz went to the state fair. Being city people, they found the farm animal displays very interesting.

"It says here," Mrs. Horowitz said, "that this bull mates over 150 times every year."

"That seems like a lot of work," stated Mr. Horowitz.

"Can you imagine, 150 times a year?" Mrs. Horowitz asked.

"Sure I can imagine," Mr. Horowitz nodded, "I bet he does it with 150 different ladies."

410. ☆☆☆☆☆☆☆☆

David Epstein was the love of his parents, amazingly smart, but a real thorn in the side of every teacher he had. After being called to the principal's office for the eighth time, it was suggested that David complete his fourth grade experience at a different school.

Out of desperation, the Epsteins enrolled David in the Catholic school with a reputation for academic excellence and old fashioned nun discipline.

At the end of the first day, the reports were all positive. At the end of the first week, the teachers sent home glowing accolades about how well David was doing. At the end of the first month, David was awarded student of the month due to his academic performance!

Not meaning to rock the boat, the Epsteins sat David down to find out what was going on.

"David," his father asked, "your mother and I are so happy with how well you are doing at the new Catholic school... but, we don't understand... how come?"

"Do you know the large statue of that guy in the front hall of the school? The one that is nailed to the cross?"

"Yes."

"Nails through his hands and his feet."

"Yes."

"He has a thing of barbed wire wrapped around his forehead."

"Yes."

"He has stab marks in his side."

"Yes."

"You know that he's Jewish like me?"

"Yes!"

"Well, they love him, think what they'd do to me!"

411. ☆ ☆ ☆ ☆ ☆ ☆ ☆ ☆ ☆ ☆

From the perspective of my dog, a parking meter is a pay toilet that the car isn't using correctly.

412. ☆ ☆ ☆ ☆ ☆ ☆ ☆ ☆ ☆ ☆

When I was a child I got into trouble for asking too many questions in Sunday School. Sister Mary was telling us about how handsome Adam was and how beautiful Eve was when I asked, "Sister, where did all the ugly people come from?"

413. ☆ ☆ ☆ ☆ ☆ ☆ ☆ ☆ ☆ ☆

Bob noticed a lovely coed while he was studying at the library. Looking for some reason to talk to her, he walked by where she was studying. "Hi, sorry to interrupt, but I couldn't help but notice what you are reading."

"Oh, yes," she smiled. "This is a fascinating book about human sexuality."

"Really?" Bob sat down.

"Yeah, for example it states that statistically, Native Americans and Polish men are the best lovers."

"Nice to meet you," Bob said as he reached his hand across the table. "My name is Running Feather Kowalski."

414. ☆ ☆ ☆ ☆ ☆ ☆ ☆ ☆ ☆

A very posh school gave a scholarship to a kindergarden age boy from the inner city. On the first day of school the new student went to his teacher and said, "I ain't got no crayons."

"Tyrone," the teacher gently corrected, "you mean to say, 'I don't have any crayons.' Or you can say, 'we don't have any crayons' 'they don't have any crayons.' Do you understand what I am teaching you?"

"Sure," said Tyrone, "You don't know what happened to all the fuckin' crayons neither."

415. ☆ ☆ ☆ ☆ ☆ ☆ ☆ ☆ ☆

A drunk woman was not satisfied with the performance of her one-night stand. "How disappointing. Your organ was just too small!"

"It only seemed small," growled the drunk man, "because you asked it to play in a cathedral!"

416. ☆ ☆ ☆ ☆ ☆ ☆ ☆ ☆ ☆

Lenny was a little fearful of girls, but he decided he had to have sex. "High school is over and I don't want to go to college a virgin," he told himself.

So Lenny mustered up the guts to sneak out of the house and rode his bike to the red light district of town. Once there, he met a kindly woman who seemed to instinctively know Lenny's predicament.

"It's OK Ducky, she said. "Let Marla teach you the ropes. You just come down this alley with Marla, come on little Ducky."

Marla leaned up against the wall in the shadows of the alley and hitched up her dress. "Just stick it in there," she said, "it'll be just fine."

Lenny did what he was told and he seemed to be getting the swing of things when he got concerned.

"Am I doing it right?" Lenny asked. "You seem to be nodding your head a lot."

"It's nothing, Ducky, she said, "you just tucked the end of my scarf in, that's all."

417. ☆ ☆ ☆ ☆ ☆ ☆ ☆ ☆ ☆

Texans often are portrayed in jokes as showoffs and braggers. So let's keep this tradition going...

Why don't they make toilet paper in Texas?
Because a Texan won't take shit off of nobody!

418. ☆ ☆ ☆ ☆ ☆ ☆ ☆ ☆ ☆

Two sons of Texas were visiting San Francisco. They found themselves walking across the famous Golden Gate Bridge late one night.

"Man do I need to pee like a racehorse," one said.

"Me too," said the other. "Let's whizz off the side of this here bridge."

The first o ne relieved himself and said, "Damn this water is cold!"

The second added, "And deep too!"

419. ☆ ☆ ☆ ☆ ☆ ☆ ☆ ☆ ☆

Bob, a kind and gentle older fellow, walked into work with a huge black eye.

"What happened Bob?" his coworker Mary asked.

"A lady at church punched me in the eye."

"At church?" Mary asked.

"Yeah," Bob said. "I was at Sunday service and we all stood to sing out of the hymnal. I happened to notice that the plump woman in front of me had her dress stuck in her... you know... cheeks. So I politely pulled on her dress so that she wouldn't be embarrassed."

"Is that when you got slugged?" asked Mary.

"No," Bob explained, "she just turned around and gave me a stern look so I thought she wanted her dress tucked back in. So I carefully wedged it back in. That's when she slugged me!"

When telling this joke, it is best to use hand gestures as you "carefully wedge the dress back in."

420. ☆ ☆ ☆ ☆ ☆ ☆ ☆ ☆ ☆

Old Mr. Goldstein went to a whorehouse and said. "I'd like a nice girl, with big boobs, and red hair if you have one."

"We sure do sir," said the madam. "That will be $200."

"$200 dollars! You're putting me on!"

"Sure, but that'll be another fifty dollars."

421. ☆ ☆ ☆ ☆ ☆ ☆ ☆ ☆ ☆

Mr. Goldstein was 84 years old but still went to work everyday. He would joke to friends, "I wake up in the morning, and check the obituaries. If my name isn't in it, I open up the Playboy magazine to get my heart pumping faster— then I get out of bed."

422. ☆ ☆ ☆ ☆ ☆ ☆ ☆ ☆ ☆

Mr. Steel was a cattle rancher. He had built a thriving business producing and shipping beef around the world.

At a charity event, Mr. Steel, wearing his ten gallon hat, white suit, and alligator shoes met Mr. Goldstein, who was a slight man, wearing an old suit, and well worn loafers.

"Ya know I have the largest spread in Maverick County," Mr. Steel bragged. "150 thousand acres of prime grazing land. You can ride all day in one of my gold Cadillacs and still not see the whole spread."

"That's nice," said Mr. Goldstein.

"Yep, I herd 20 thousand head of prime cattle, what a sight... Yep, what a sight," Mr. Steel said.

"That's nice," said Mr. Goldstein.

"Yes sir, 150 thousand acres of Texas, now that is something to see."

"That's nice," said Mr. Goldstein.

"Do you own any land?" Mr. Steel asked. "A man should own his own land… I'm sure you would agree."

"Yes. I own a little land," said Mr. Goldstein.

"Good for you. A man can't call himself a real man if he don't own himself at least a couple hundred acres to call his own. I branded my land, Steel Ranch, what do you call your parcel?"

"Oh, I don't own that much," said Mr. Goldstein. "I guess it's called 18 acres of downtown Dallas."

423. ☆ ☆ ☆ ☆ ☆ ☆ ☆ ☆

Mr. Brodsky was 96 years old. He lived independently until last month when he took an awful fall and broke his hip. (Poor fellow, but he will be fine.) His four children were concerned how he was doing in the Jewish Nursing Home so they went to see him.

"Poppa," the oldest boy said. "Are they treating you well here?"

"It's nice here they treat me like I'm a king. A king I say. The staff are very attentive to my every need."

As he was talking he started to list a little to the left. And then, like an angel, this nice nurse swooped in and gently straightened Mr. Brodsky up and put a red velvet pillow under his left elbow.

"The food is amazing," Mr. Brodsky continued. "It's as if my own beloved mother, God rest her soul, was cooking my every meal."

Then Mr. Brodsky started to list to the other side and a different nurse came out of nowhere and gently straightened him up and placed another red velvet pillow under his right arm.

"I only have one real complaint," Mr. Brodsky said. "They won't let me fart!"

424. ☆☆☆☆☆☆☆☆☆

The Great Leberwitz had a long career in burlesque. He did his show for over 40 years just off the main street at Coney Island. A few jokes, a little magic, and juggling. But it was his finale that separated him from the other showman of his day.

Max was so excited when he heard that The Great Leberwitz was doing a charity event in Miami.

"You've got to see this guy," Max told his friend. "He's amazing, especially the thing he does with the walnuts."

The Great Leberwitz did his show and it was just as Max remembered. Then came the big finish. The Great Leberwitz came out on stage dressed in a red silk dressing gown. In front of him was a sturdy wood table. The Great Leberwitz carefully put three coconuts on the table lined up just right. Then he opened his robe. He lifted his enormous manhood up like a sledgehammer and WHAM, WHAM, WHAM… the three coconuts were smashed to smithereens. The crowd gave him a standing ovation.

Max went backstage to meet The Great Leberwitz.

"Mr. Leberwitz, I'm a big fan," Max gushed. "I saw you when I was a kid in New York. How come you're using coconuts now?"

The Great Leberwitz shrugged, "My sight, it ain't what it used to be."

425. ☆ ☆ ☆ ☆ ☆ ☆ ☆ ☆ ☆

A rich city kid attended Wyoming State. He was a nice enough kid, but boy did he complain a lot. Nothing pleased him.

"Back home the pizza is the best." "It's so quiet here it's hard to sleep." "Back home the girls are more sophisticated."

The night of the fall barn dance his roommates were just sick and tired of his complaints. They decided that they were going to prank him so he couldn't ruin the big shindig.

They got him to come behind the barn, then they jumped him. They put a gag in his mouth and a burlap bag over his head. They stripped him stark naked and tied him to a tree.

"You bitch so much, we've decided you don't get to go to the barn dance," his roommates told him. "You hang out here and enjoy the music and we'll come get you later."

They were going to leave him there for only a little while, but the party was a blast and they forgot all about him. The music was good and the beer was flowing. At 4 in the morning they realized that they had left him tied to a tree for over 9 hours. They ran behind the barn to find their friend all dehydrated. He was all skin and bones and bent over limp. He looked dead.

"Are you OK?" they yelled as they removed the hood and the gag. "Someone get him some water! Are you OK?"

In a low worn out voice the city kid said, "Doesn't that calf have a mother?"

426.   ☆ ☆ ☆ ☆ ☆ ☆ ☆ ☆ ☆

Why don't unmarried women pass gas?
Because they don't get an asshole until they're married.

427.   ☆ ☆ ☆ ☆ ☆ ☆ ☆ ☆ ☆

According to my Aunt Sadie, "Women don't pass gas, but sometimes they stand by a dog that does."

428.   ☆ ☆ ☆ ☆ ☆ ☆ ☆ ☆ ☆

Mr. Goldblat was dying. He called his lawyer, his doctor, and his rabbi to his death bed. He wanted to make sure that they each understood the solemn oath they had made to him.

"When I am laid to rest, I expect each of you to put one-third of my money in my coffin with me. I have the bags over there, each with $100,000 in thousand dollar bills in them. I earned it and I want to take it with me."

A few days later the three men were at the funeral, each in turn placed the money into the coffin.

That night the three men were discussing the day over drinks. The rabbi said, "Such a selfish man, his money could have helped so many needy in this world."

The doctor said, "The thought of all that money in neat thousand dollor bills just rotting in the earth like that just sickens me."

A few minutes later the rabbi said to the lawyer, "You don't seem so bothered about all that money going to waste."

"I'm not bothered at all, it's his money. He can do what he wants with it," said the lawyer. "When no one was looking I took all the money and left him a check."

429.   ☆ ☆ ☆ ☆ ☆ ☆ ☆ ☆ ☆

Harold and Maude had been married for 52 years. One night he woke her up and excitedly said, "Maude it's a miracle. I was making pishy and God illuminated the toilet. It was a miracle I tell you!"

"Oh Harold, you peed in the refrigerator again."

430. ☆ ☆ ☆ ☆ ☆ ☆ ☆ ☆ ☆

A blind adrenaline junkie was telling a small group about his exploits.

"I think the biggest rush for me was last summer when I went sky diving."

"You sky dive?" A man asked. "Weren't you afraid you were't going to pull the cord soon enough?"

"Nah," said the blind guy. "But it did scare the b-jesus out of my dog."

431. ☆ ☆ ☆ ☆ ☆ ☆ ☆ ☆ ☆

Jake and Jimmy were best friends and flight mechanics for a small airline based in Nevada. One day, they were bemoaning that their money had run out before the month did.

"I can't believe it, we don't have anything to drink for 2 whole days," Jake complained.

"I heard that you can cut jet fuel with tonic water and it's better than vodka," Jimmy said.

So after work they snuck a gallon of the expensive jet fuel out of the fuel depot and got completely shit faced in the field behind the maintenance hanger.

When Jimmy woke up the next morning, he had a splitting headache and he couldn't find his buddy, Jake.

His cell phone rang and it was Jake.

"Jake," Jimmy asked, "you didn't drive home, did ya?"

"No, I'm in California," Jake said.

"What are you doing in California?"

"Well Jimmy, when I woke up I had a splitting headache…"

"Me too, but I still don't get why you're in California?"

"Well Jimmy," Jake said. "I hope you don't need to fart."

432.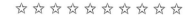

In one of those southern states, there was a good old boy with no arms, who came to a house of ill repute. For all of you not so educated types, that's fancy talk for whorehouse.

The madam opened the door and saw he was short two arms. Not wanting to be indelicate she said, "Are you sure you're ready to take on one of my girls?"

"Yes ma'am," he said with a smile. "I figure the biggest test was ringing that there door bell."

433.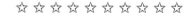

Mr. Wandsworth was a dignified older gentleman who was in the hospital because of chest pain.

"How am I doing?" Mr. Wandsworth asked his doctor. "Give it to me straight. I can handle the truth."

"Well, Mr. Wandsworth," the young internist said, "don't buy any green bananas."

434. ☆ ☆ ☆ ☆ ☆ ☆ ☆ ☆ ☆ ☆

Now, a bedtime story:

There was a kingdom which had the strange custom of picking their king based on, how do we say this politely, manhood size.

As it turned out, there were some newlyweds that were getting frisky in a small village in the southern most part of this kingdom. The wife pointed out with great glee, "Wow, beloved husband, you are huge. Are you bigger than the king?"

"I don't know," said the new husband. "Let's measure."

When a ruler was not long enough the new wife went and got a yard stick, for they wanted an accurate measurement.

"14 ¼ inches long," squealed the new wife. "That has to be the biggest one eyed monster in the land!"

The next day, the couple started on their long journey to the capital. When they arrived they went straight to the King's castle and knocked on the giant doors.

A small window in the left door opened, and an old man stuck his head out.

"Yeah, what do you two want?" he said as he looked down upon them.

"I would like to be officially measured for the job of the King," said the young man.

"OK, young man, how large do you reckon you be?" asked the old man in the window.

"I'm 14 and ¼ inches," said the young man.

"Really, you're 14 and ¼ inches long," the old man repeated with astonishment. "You said, over 14… I don't believe you!" and he started to laugh as he slammed the window.

The couple stood out in front of the giant wooden doors listening to the man from the window unlocking and grunting as the giant doors opened.

The old man walked out with 6 royal guards and stood in front of the couple. He pulled up his pant leg and said. "You see the bulge the size of an apple in my sock?"

"Yes," they both nodded.

"And, I'm just the door man!"

435. ☆ ☆ ☆ ☆ ☆ ☆ ☆ ☆ ☆

Mr. Rosenthal was brought into the emergency room with a ghastly gash on his head.

"What happened?" the attending doctor said as he applied pressure to slow the bleeding.

"My wife has gained a few pounds so she decided to get a little exercise playing golf with me. I was showing her how to improve her game and she was in good humor.

"Then she hit a dog leg that sent her ball into a pasture. So we went to find it. My Becky had a little trouble getting through the fence, but she was being good natured about the whole weight thing.

"I found her ball right smack under the tail of this humongous cow. This behemoth refused to move, so I grabbed her tail and I lifted with all my might.

"I pointed to Becky's ball and said, 'Sweetheart, this one looks like yours.' And for no reason she walloped me with a 9 iron."

436. ☆ ☆ ☆ ☆ ☆ ☆ ☆ ☆ ☆

Bob and Harold were waiting in line at the bank when the robbers yelled, "This is a hold up!"

The masked thugs were robbing the bank with military precision.

"All you people in line, get out your money and hold it over your head. When I come by with the bag, drop it in."

Bob stuck $40 in Harold's hand and said, "Here's the money I borrowed from you last week."

437. ☆ ☆ ☆ ☆ ☆ ☆ ☆ ☆ ☆

A prestigious law firm was trying to hire a new lawyer. The competition was stiff, so the senior partners devised a character test for the 3 most qualified applicants.

They invited each candidate back for a final interview. At the end of the interview each candidate was given a manilla envelope and told, "Here is some historical information about our illustrious firm. Please read it at your leisure."

When the candidates left the office, each found no historical information in the envelope. Only ten, newly printed, one thousand dollar bills.

The first lady returned the money before the close of business. The second lady returned the money first thing the next morning. The third woman never returned a dime.

Which attorney did the prestigious law firm hire?

The answer, the one with the biggest tits.

438. ☆ ☆ ☆ ☆ ☆ ☆ ☆ ☆ ☆

A giraffe walks into a bar and announces at the top of his lungs, "The high balls are on me!"

439. ☆ ☆ ☆ ☆ ☆ ☆ ☆ ☆ ☆

Mr. Ginsberg had been a widow for a long time and he was feeling very lonely. He decided he was going to ask the lovely waitress from the Chinese restaurant he frequented on a date. In spite of her being Chinese and much younger than him, the two hit it off.

One night the evening turned to romance and the couple made whoop-ti doop-ti until the sun came up. While they were cuddling, she said how much she enjoyed his tenderness and asked if there was anything she could do to make him happy.

Mr. Ginsberg was feeling a little adventurous and confessed that he had never tried, but would really like to try, some 69.

She got furious and bolted out of bed, grabbing her clothes up from around the room. "After all your romancing," she yelled. "You really are just a chauvinist pig! You think I should bring you pleasure in bed and then stir you up some Broccoli and Beef!"

440.   ☆ ☆ ☆ ☆ ☆ ☆ ☆ ☆ ☆

Mr. Rosenthal was a fixture at the golf course. All that knew him could attest, he loved the game of golf. One day on the 17th hole, a funeral precession drove by. Mr. Rosenthal took off his hat and stood at attention with his hand on his heart. After a few minutes, he returned his gaze back to the ball.

His oldest friend said, "Arty, who's funeral was that?"

"Oh, didn't I tell you, that was Becky… God rest her soul. She made my life heaven-on-earth for the last 42 years."

441.   ☆ ☆ ☆ ☆ ☆ ☆ ☆ ☆ ☆

Ruth Ollins said. "Dwn wth vwls."

442.   ☆ ☆ ☆ ☆ ☆ ☆ ☆ ☆ ☆

A drag queen, after a night of drinking, stumbled into a Catholic church early Sunday morning. Teetering down the aisle he ran smack into the priest who was preforming the ceremony.

"I'm sorry honey," the queen said. "I love the dress, but your handbag's on fire."

443.   ☆ ☆ ☆ ☆ ☆ ☆ ☆ ☆ ☆

I have been married to a teacher for about 25 years so I hear a lot of stories concerning schools and teachers. In my area, for the last 15 years, the schools have been woefully underfunded. The schools are struggling along trying to make ends meet, but it is not going well. With class size issues and limited space one year my wife taught in the hallway off of the library. This situation brought me to the following cartoon:

For a cartoonist, the hall of fame is getting your work onto someone's refrigerator. This may sound silly, but I love it when someone tells me they put one of my cartoons onto their icebox. (I know it's like a kindergartner's finger painting, but I still like it!) I was amazingly flattered when I spied the above cartoon posted in the staff room at the Shasta County Office of Education.

444.   ☆ ☆ ☆ ☆ ☆ ☆ ☆ ☆ ☆

A visitor to Chicago was very excited to go to the top of a skyscraper. He really wanted to see what there was to see and to experience the famous windiness of the great city.

On top he interrupted a couple having an elegant lunch of fancy sandwiches and a bottle of fine wine.

"Isn't this great," the visitor said, "the wind is so strong I find myself fearful of being blown off."

The gentleman sipped his wine and said, "Sir, you are very safe. Have a nice day."

Not noticing that the couple wanted to be alone, the visitor continued. "What a view! What a wind!"

"Sir, the gentleman said. "You are very safe up here. In fact the wind is so strong that if you did fall off this roof, the wind would simply deposit you on the 110th floor."

"Really?" the visitor said. "You're pulling my leg."

At that, the gentleman threw himself off the roof. The visitor looked over the edge and saw the gentleman climbing in through an open window somewhere around the 110th floor.

A few moments later the gentleman stepped off the elevator and the visitor said, "That was amazing. I want to do it." Then he jumped off the roof.

The visitor fell to his death.

As the gentleman sat down and picked up his glass, the lady said, "Sometimes Clark Kent you can be a real asshole!"

445.   ☆ ☆ ☆ ☆ ☆ ☆ ☆ ☆ ☆

Robert was top of his class in business school and he was very excited when he was offered an amazing position with Microsoft.

After only 3 months of working at Microsoft, he got invited to a fancy corporate party at Mr. Gate's house. It was like in the movies—lavish, elegant, and opulent.

The next morning he found himself behind the pool house, partially clothed, and sporting a mind splitting hangover. He couldn't remember a thing except for how impressed he was with Mr. Gates' elegant mansion.

A few months later he ended up in an elevator with Mr. Gates. He found himself nervous and tongue tied, and he knew he sounded stupid even as he said it, "I was so impressed with your lovely home, Mr. Gates. Even the toilet was amazing, all gold and shiny."

"That is very kind of you young man," Mr. Gates said, "and I think I have finally figured out who shit in my tuba."

446.   ☆ ☆ ☆ ☆ ☆ ☆ ☆ ☆ ☆

Mr. Horowitz was very concerned for his wife. For years she was a kleptomaniac. Today she was in front of the judge because of a shoplifting charge.

"Mrs. Horowitz, I don't know what I'm going to do with you. This must be the tenth time you have been in my court. What did you steal?

"A can of peaches, your honor," she said as she started to cry.

"And how many peaches were in the can?" the judge asked.

"I think six, why do you want to know such a thing?"

"Well Mrs. Horowitz, you will have to go to jail for six days," said the judge.

"Your honor, sir," Mr. Horowitz yelled from the back of the courtroom, "Last week she also stole a can of peas."

447. ☆☆☆☆☆☆☆☆☆

A very large man was sitting next to an attractive woman on a plane. After a little chitchat, the woman politely said, "I don't wish to be indelicate, you seem very kind, but I just want you to know I am happily married."

The rotund man let out a massive sigh and said, "Thank you for telling me. I don't think I could have held my stomach in all the way to Boise."

448. ☆☆☆☆☆☆☆☆☆

This next joke is very popular with men that are going through a divorce.

A county sheriff in Texas spied a fancy car going well over 100 miles per hour. He lit off after the fancy car, and for 20 minutes they sped all over creation hitting top speeds of 120 miles per hour.

Then, to the sheriff's surprise, the fancy car slowed down and finally stopped.

The sheriff sauntered up to the driver and said, "What in tarnation was that all about!"

"I'm sorry sheriff, I didn't know it was you."

"Me? What you taking about boy!"

"Well sir," The nervous driver explained. "About ten months ago my wife ran off with a cop, I was just scared to death that you were trying to bring her back."

(After the laughter add: "The sheriff let the man off with a warning.")

449. ☆ ☆ ☆ ☆ ☆ ☆ ☆ ☆ ☆ ☆

George and Max have been best friends since the first day of kindergarten. Nowadays they go to different colleges, so for spring break they decide to go backpacking in the wilderness.

They drive Max's Jeep to the middle of the Sierras and proceed to pack in for seven days of backcountry adventure.

A few hours into their trek, George steps off the trail to relieve himself. Then it happens. A rattlesnake is not happy about being disturbed and lashes out, bitting poor George right on the end of his manhood.

George is in agony and Max is petrified for his friend. Holding his fear under control, Max decides he better run back to the Jeep and call for emergency help.

As fast as he can traverse the terrain, Max returns to the Jeep. He gets hold of emergency dispatch on the CB radio.

"It is very important you do exactly what I say," the dispatcher warns. "You need to get to your friend as quickly as possible and cut small X's directly over the fang marks. Then you must suck the venom out. Make sure you do not swallow any of the venom. We will be there in about three hours. Go now and hopefully you can save your friend's life."

Max runs back to George in record time. He finds George breathing shallowly, his skin is ashen. He is holding his groin and seems to be in great agony.

"I got ahold of emergency dispatch," Max huffed and puffed.

"What did they say?" George whispers.

Max knelt down next to George, "They said you're going to die."

450. ☆ ☆ ☆ ☆ ☆ ☆ ☆ ☆

A teenage gymnast went to confession.

"Forgive me Father for I have sinned. I allowed a classmate to touch me inappropriately and I had impure thoughts."

After a discussion about appropriate behavior, the priest gave her penance and told her 'to sin no more'.

The guilt ridden gymnast was so relieved by getting absolution that she ran down the center of the church and did a few cartwheels out of pure joy.

Two women, waiting their turn for Confession, saw the girl's behavior and were shocked.

One turned to the other and said, "Father O'Leary is giving out difficult penance today."

"My, my, yes," the other woman said. "And of all the days for me not to be wearing any undies."

451. ☆ ☆ ☆ ☆ ☆ ☆ ☆ ☆ ☆

P.J. O'Rourke said, "Drugs have taught an entire generation of kids the metric system."

452. ☆ ☆ ☆ ☆ ☆ ☆ ☆ ☆ ☆

Two older bulls and a teenage bull were talking on top of a hill. The two older bulls were not happy that the farmer was bringing in a new bull.

"I don't like it!" one bull said.

"That's the way it is, we'll just have to fight the new guy to see who gets to mate," the other stated.

The little bull said, "I don't care what you guys say I'm not giving up any of my herd to a newcomer."

The older bulls smiled at him then noticed some commotion coming up the farm road. It was hard to tell for sure, but it looked like a humungous bull was smashing and denting a semi-truck trailer from the inside. As the truck got closer, their fears were proven. The trailer of the semi was lurching from side to side and loud grunts were echoing throughout the farm. It looked like a diabolical bovine was coming to their quiet farm.

One bull said to the other, "I think we should be open minded, welcome him in, and not be disagreeable."

The other bull readily agreed.

The little bull started pawing at the ground and snorting up a storm.

"What, are you nuts? You're going to fight that behemoth?"

"Hell no!" said the little fellow. "I just want to make sure he knows I'm a fucking bull!"

453. ☆ ☆ ☆ ☆ ☆ ☆ ☆ ☆ ☆

A bull and a teenage bull were grazing on top of a hill watching over a large herd. The young bull said, "I think I'm going to charge down there and have sex with one of them there cows."

"Not me," said the older fellow. "I'm going to walk on down there and <u>fuck</u> all of 'em!"

454. ☆☆☆☆☆☆☆☆

My wife was in labor so I called the hospital.
The nurse said, "Calm down, is this her first child?"
"No," I said, "this is her husband."

455. ☆☆☆☆☆☆☆☆

A grandson had to go visit his grandmother when he was home during college break. He wasn't looking forward to it but he had to visit her.

After a few minutes of chitchat, the phone rang and his grandmother went to the kitchen to answer it. While she was gone he enjoyed a few peanuts from a fancy bowl on the coffee table.

When the grandma returned he was a little embarrassed.

"I'm sorry grandma, but while I was waiting I ate all of your peanuts.

"That's OK," she smiled. "Because of my dentures, I can only suck the chocolate off 'em."

456. ☆☆☆☆☆☆☆☆

Dr. Goldfarb was a renown psychiatrist sitting at his parents' Thanksgiving dinner table. He was thinking about his childhood and life in their grand house. Old memories floated through his consciousness.

"Mom you ruined my life," he said. "You stifled me at every turn. You were emasculating and hateful."

His mother was shocked, "What... what did you say?"

"I'm so sorry, mother," he said. "That was a Freudian slip. What I meant to say was, 'Please pass the peas.'"

457. ☆☆☆☆☆☆☆☆

Little Bobby was running around and playing when he trotted into the barn. He saw his father and a few men doing something. Little Bobby could make no sense out of what he saw, so he screamed with shock.

"It's OK Bobby," his father said. "We'll have the baby horse out of the mommy horse in no time."

"But dad!" yelled Bobby. "Just how fast was that baby horse running?"

458. ☆ ☆ ☆ ☆ ☆ ☆ ☆ ☆ ☆

Sister Mary Joseph went to confession.

"Forgive me Father for I have sinned. I was playing golf and I said the f-word 4 times."

"Well my child," said Father Murphy. "I'm sure God will understand. Tell me what happened so you can learn from your mistakes."

"I was teeing off the first hole and I sliced it. I was so shocked, the F-word just popped out."

"Yes my child," Father Murphy consoled.

"Then I hit it right into a sand trap. After four terrible attempts I just lost it and let loose another F-bomb," said Sister Mary Joseph.

"Yes my child," Father Murphy consoled.

"On top of everything, I went from the sand trap right into the pond. Again I said that awful word."

"Yes my child," Father Murphy consoled.

"I prayed for help from the All Mighty and my game got dramatically better. I was tied for first with my friend, Sister Margaret at the last hole. It was a simple 3 foot putt for the win, and..."

"No!" Father Murphy interrupted. "Don't tell me you missed the fucking 3 foot putt!"

459. ☆ ☆ ☆ ☆ ☆ ☆ ☆ ☆ ☆

My sister was in her late twenties and our mother was very concerned that she wasn't married. One day I overheard them arguing.

"I can't go out with him again, now that I know he's a transvestite!" Sis said.

"You shouldn't be so picky," mom screamed. "In fact, you should marry him, you'll double your wardrobe!"

"Now when you leave you lock every other one. When the burglar is picking 'em he'll always be locking half."

460. ☆ ☆ ☆ ☆ ☆ ☆ ☆ ☆ ☆ ☆

One of my patients was thrown out of a mime show because he was having a seizure.

They thought he was heckling.

461. ☆ ☆ ☆ ☆ ☆ ☆ ☆ ☆ ☆ ☆

One cannibal asked another cannibal, "Does this clown taste funny to you?"

462. ☆ ☆ ☆ ☆ ☆ ☆ ☆ ☆ ☆ ☆

One cannibal said to the another cannibal, "I don't like my mother."

"Yeah, OK. But if you're still hungry have some more mashed

potatoes instead."

463. ☆ ☆ ☆ ☆ ☆ ☆ ☆ ☆ ☆ ☆

Reginald Bluff went to the doctor, "Doctor I think I swallowed a pillow."
"How do you feel?" the doctor asked.
"A little down in the mouth."

464. ☆ ☆ ☆ ☆ ☆ ☆ ☆ ☆ ☆ ☆

What's the nicest thing a husband can say to his wife in Arkansas?
"Nice tooth."

465. ☆ ☆ ☆ ☆ ☆ ☆ ☆ ☆ ☆ ☆

Mr. Moser is new in town and he has a real problem. So he seeks out a Rabbi, "Rabbi I think my wife is poisoning my coffee."
"What a horrible thing to say about your wife," says the Rabbi.
"I know, I know, but she is poisoning my coffee," says Mr. Moser.
"Let me talk to your wife, I'm sure there is some sort of misunderstanding," says the Rabbi.
The next day, Mr. Moser met with the rabbi.
"I met your wife," said the Rabbi. "Spent almost three hours talking to her, counseling her…"
"Yeah, what should I do?"
"If I were you and married to your wife… I'd drink more of her coffee!"

466. ☆ ☆ ☆ ☆ ☆ ☆ ☆ ☆ ☆ ☆

Reginald Bluff was so happy when he won a new toilet brush in the church picnic raffle.
A few weeks later the pastor ran into Reg at the store and said, "Hey Reg, how do ya like the new toilet brush?"
"Not so much pastor, I'm going back to toilet paper."

467. ☆☆☆☆☆☆☆☆☆☆

Reg saw his wife coming up the drive with only one boot on. "What happened, you lose a boot?"

"Nope, found me one."

468. ☆☆☆☆☆☆☆☆☆☆

Reg and Vern were driving the country road back from work when they came upon an unusual sight. A female deer was stuck head first in the fence and a male deer was using this opportunity to have his way with her.

After watching this for a moment, Vern said, "I hope you don't think this too weird but I have always wanted to do that with a deer."

"It ain't for me to judge," Reg said softly. "If you want to, I won't tell anyone."

So Reg went over to the female deer, dropped his drawers and stuck his head in the fence.

469. ☆☆☆☆☆☆☆☆☆

For this joke you will need to know these words: Zayda[9] and Bubbe[10].

Zayda is a very old man with just hours to live. He is lying in his bed surrounded by his loving family.

"Is that Bubbe's strudel I can smell?" he says in a weak and gasping voice.

"Yes it is Zayda, you rest now, save your strength," said his beloved granddaughter.

"Get me a slice of Bubbe's strudel." Zayda says. "Let me go off into the afterlife with your Bubbe's heavenly strudel on my lips. Bubbe is the love of my life and she puts all her love into her strudel."

In a little bit the girl returns empty handed.

"I'm sorry Zayda, Bubbe says the strudel is for after the funeral."

470. ☆☆☆☆☆☆☆☆

A ways out of Red Bluff, there's this old mining town. The miners work hard all day and only get back to civilization about once a year.

Reg took a job out there and one night around the campfire he confessed to missing female company. One of the old timers explained that during the mining season, most of the miners took sheep as fe-

---

[9] Yiddish for grandfather.

[10] Yiddish for grandmother

male company.

"Wow, isn't that against the law?" Reg asked.

"Not around here," the old timer explained. "The sheriff is very understanding. We even have a spring dance where we dress up and dance with our lady friends."

Come spring Reg was very excited about going to the dance. He and his sheep got all dressed up and went down to the grange hall.

When Reg walked in the door all the men and most of the sheep gasped. The old timer ran over to him putting up his hands.

"Reg, what the hell are you doing?"

"What?" Reg said. "You said it was OK around these parts."

"Yeah for sure," the old timer said. "But not with the Sheriff's gal!"

Marquis de Sod

471. ☆ ☆ ☆ ☆ ☆ ☆ ☆ ☆

David Berry said, "Children are nature's very own form of birth control."

472. ☆ ☆ ☆ ☆ ☆ ☆ ☆ ☆ ☆

Charles Schultz said, "A good education is the next best thing to a pushy mother."

473. ☆ ☆ ☆ ☆ ☆ ☆ ☆ ☆ ☆

Mark left Wall Street for a more simple life of ranching in the midwest. He bought a beautiful spread for the family and him to settle down on.

His buddy Bobby flew out from New York City to visit, and Mark picked him up at the tiny airport just east of town.

"I'm so impressed that you really bought the ranch you always wanted," said Bobby. "What did you name your ranch?"

"It was great. We let the kids name the ranch. It was kind of hard for them to agree, so we finally called it the Flying Y Double D Creekside Lazy Loco Lizard Ranch."

"Wow," Bobby said. "That's quite a name. How many cattle do you have?"

"We don't have any, none survived the branding."

474. ☆ ☆ ☆ ☆ ☆ ☆ ☆ ☆ ☆

Rita Rudner said, "A man with pierced ears is better prepared for marriage. He has experienced pain and bought jewelry."

475. ☆ ☆ ☆ ☆ ☆ ☆ ☆ ☆ ☆

Yo sister is so dumb, she didn't know how to stop her brain from itching.
So I told her, "Think about sandpaper." And she said it helped!

476. ☆ ☆ ☆ ☆ ☆ ☆ ☆ ☆ ☆

Bumper snicker:

Feel safe tonight... sleep with a cop.

477. ☆ ☆ ☆ ☆ ☆ ☆ ☆ ☆ ☆

Mr. Robertson was asked by the divorce court judge, "Before I can grant your divorce I need to know at least one specific reason that proves that you and your wife have irreconcilable differences."
"Well, your honor," Mr. Robertson said, "I don't really have one specific problem with my wife. It's just that I don't seem to get along well with her boyfriends."

478. ☆ ☆ ☆ ☆ ☆ ☆ ☆ ☆ ☆

A guy walked into a psychiatrist's office and said in a booming voice, "I think I am God!"
"Interesting," said the psychiatrist. "When did this start?"
"Well first I made the sun, and I was feeling pretty good. Then I made the…"

479. ☆ ☆ ☆ ☆ ☆ ☆ ☆ ☆ ☆

This guy walked into a psychiatrist's office and said, "Life feels like a bottomless pit."

"That's OK," said the psychiatrist, "We'll get to the bottom of this."

480. ☆☆☆☆☆☆☆☆☆

The Pope called an emergency meeting of the Council of Cardinals in the middle of the night. This had not happened in over 600 years.

The gathering showed concern on their faces as the Pope entered the Great Hall holding a piece of paper.

"I have some good news and some bad news," said the Pope. "Our Lord and Savior, Jesus Christ, has returned."

"That is good news," said one of the cardinals. "What is the bad news?"

Holding up the single piece of paper the Pope said, "This email is from Salt Lake City."

481. ☆☆☆☆☆☆☆☆☆

For the math geeks among us.

As you probably know, "milli" is the Latin suffix for one thousandth of something, such as the tiny unit of time called a millisecond.

With this in mind, Helen of Troy supposedly had "a face that could launch a thousand ships." Thus, if someone only had a face that could launch a single ship, that would be a "millihelen".

482. ☆☆☆☆☆☆☆☆☆

Patrick Murray said, "Teenagers are God's punishment for having sex."

483. ☆☆☆☆☆☆☆☆☆

Rodney Dangerfield said, "If her dress had pockets my wife would look like a pool table."

484. ☆ ☆ ☆ ☆ ☆ ☆ ☆ ☆ ☆

This guy, all covered in gold paint, walked into a psychiatrist's office.

The psychiatrist looked him all over and said, "It seems you have a gilt complex."

485. ☆ ☆ ☆ ☆ ☆ ☆ ☆ ☆ ☆

A man walked into a bar, rubbed his head, and said "Ow!"

486. ☆ ☆ ☆ ☆ ☆ ☆ ☆ ☆ ☆

A Jew walked into a bar, rubbed his head, and said "Oy!"

487. ☆ ☆ ☆ ☆ ☆ ☆ ☆ ☆ ☆

A horse walked into a bar and the bartender said, "Hey, what's with the long face?"

488. ☆ ☆ ☆ ☆ ☆ ☆ ☆ ☆ ☆

A bear walked into a bar and asked the bartender.

"Are .... these .... peanuts .... for .... any .... one?"

The bartender said, "Hey, what's with the large paws?"

"At first I was pretty self conscious, then I saw the ads the Gynecology Department has to wear."

489.   ☆ ☆ ☆ ☆ ☆ ☆ ☆ ☆ ☆ ☆

Two old friends are out walking their dogs.

"You want to stop for a drink?" the first asked.

"Sure, but I don't want to leave Rover tied outside in this heat," the second friend said.

"Yeah, OK. I have a plan. Just keep your sunglasses on and act blind.

The first man strolled confidently into the bar and got served. The second man decided to try the same trick and started towards the bar.

The bartender yelled out, "What are you doing Mac? No dogs allowed in this bar."

"But I'm blind…"

The bartender interrupted him. "Blind my ass, that dog's a Chihuahua!"

The second man looked shocked and yelled. "They gave me a Chihuahua?"

490. ☆ ☆ ☆ ☆ ☆ ☆ ☆ ☆ ☆

W.C. Fields said, "Beauty is in the eyes of the beer-holder."

491. ☆ ☆ ☆ ☆ ☆ ☆ ☆ ☆ ☆

A mugger jumped out of the bushes wheedling a gun, and demanded money from my Aunt Sadie.

"I don't got no money," said Aunt Sadie. "It's the Sabbath and I'm just coming from synagogue."

"I know all you Jewish woman have lots of money," the mugger growled.

So he stuck his gun in his belt and with both hands he rifled through Aunt Sadie's clothes. He checked her brassier and even her panties.

"Where's your money lady, I know all you Jews are rich."

"Well," Aunt Sadie said, "if you do that for a few more minutes maybe I'll write you a check."

492. ☆ ☆ ☆ ☆ ☆ ☆ ☆ ☆ ☆

Pastor Bob was a little perturbed that his congregation was putting so little into the collection plate on Sundays. So, he decided to use hypnosis to "encourage" tithing.

Sunday after Sunday, Pastor Bob swung his grandfather's gold pocket watch in front of the congregation and in a monotone he repeated "give… give."

This worked out very well at first. Every week the collection plate was full. Then one Sunday morning Paster Bob was hypnotizing his congregation and the old watch chain broke, without thinking Pastor Bob blurted out, "Oh crap!"

493.

Red Bluff was sitting in the He's Not Here bar on the outskirts of town when Jesus walked in looking very hot and tired. Looking at the barkeep, Red said, "Give him a beer on me."

Jesus enjoyed the beer and was fixin' to leave when he noticed Red had a cane and his leg was propped up on a chair.

Jesus bent over to touch Red's bad leg when Red got up in a rush waving his arms and stumbling backwards, "Jesus, don't touch me! I'm getting disability!"

494.

A man was sitting at the bar when he heard a soft voice.
"You look very nice today."
He looked around but saw no one.
"Nice tie, good color for you."
Still no one.
"You're staying fit, you must work out a lot."
Then he realized that the voice was coming from the bowl of peanuts.
The man said to the barkeep, the peanuts are talking to me."
"Yeah, I know," said the bartender. "They're complimentary."

495.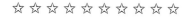

This was my Aunt Sadie's favorite joke:

It was a crowded theater on Broadway, just minutes before the show was scheduled to start. A scream from the balcony got everyone's attention.

"Is there a doctor in the house?" yelled a woman. "Is there a doctor in the house?"

Down in the expensive orchestra area three men stood up.

The woman yelled down to them, "If one of you handsome doctors is single... would you like to meet a lovely Jewish girl from a nice family?"

496. ☆ ☆ ☆ ☆ ☆ ☆ ☆ ☆ ☆

A carnival was in town and lots of people came out to see the spectacle. In one tent there was the Amazing Waldo, the world's strongest man.

First the Amazing Waldo took a large piece of pipe and placed it on his head. He pulled down on both sides, and with grunts and gritted teeth, he bent the pipe around his own head. The crowd went wild.

Next he took a thick phonebook and ripped it in half using only his teeth and one hand. The crowd screamed with amazement.

Then he took a drinking glass and placed it on a stool. With practiced showmanship he presented a lemon to the crowd.

"With my weakest hand," the Amazing Waldo announced, "I will fill this glass." As all watched in silence the Amazing Waldo crushed the lemon with his left hand and easily filled the glass.

"Now with my right hand I will get every last drop..." With powerful grunts and rippling muscles, the Amazing Waldo did as he said he would.

With sweat pouring down his face, the Amazing Waldo held up the remains of the lemon and challenged the crowd.

"I will give $100 to anyone who can get another drop out of the corpse of this lemon." The crowed cheered for the Amazing Waldo.

Then a hush came over the crowd as they realized there was this little old man slowly climbing up the steps to the stage to take on the challenge.

The little old man, took the dregs of the lemon from the Amazing Waldo, and with little ado, squeezed the dry fiber and got 4 drops to drip out. The crowd stood in stunned silence.

"Ya want more?" the old man said with a thick Yiddish accent. "For $1000 I'll give you more."

The Amazing Waldo was slack jawed and nodded his approval.

Then the old man put the lemon dregs in his right hand and forced out at least a half a glass of juice.

"That's incredible," said the Amazing Waldo. "How did you do that?"

"Oy, that was nothing," said the old man. "Before I retired I was the chief fundraiser for Temple Beth Israel.

Depending where you tell this joke you can change the name of the group and the characteristics of the old man to fit your audience. I once told this joke to the parents' group at an all girls Christian high school. I changed the hero to Sister Margaret, the school's actual representative for fundraising. The audience, and Sister Margaret loved it. I heard later that the story got told and retold throughout the school year which helped with Sister Margaret's fundraising efforts.

497. ☆ ☆ ☆ ☆ ☆ ☆ ☆ ☆

How do you make a Rottweilers?
Cross a puma with a pig.

Rottweiler owners hate this joke. We German Shepherd owners love telling this joke to Rottweiler owners.

498. ☆ ☆ ☆ ☆ ☆ ☆ ☆ ☆ ☆

Jake and Lillie met in a club in Las Vegas. After a whirlwind weekend of romance, they got married.

Returning to Jake's house in Los Angeles the romance continued. The next morning, Jake was getting ready to leave at the crack of dawn.

"Where are you going, Jake?" Lillie said sleepily.

"Lillie my love," Jake said, "I need to tell you the truth. I didn't bring it up because I didn't want you to worry, but... I'm an avid golfer. I golf almost every morning. I'm sorry for not telling you."

"I understand," said Lillie. "I too need to confess. I'm a hooker."

"Oh, that's OK," Jake smiled. "You're probably holding your grip too tight."

499. ☆ ☆ ☆ ☆ ☆ ☆ ☆ ☆ ☆

Roberto went to the owner of the circus and asked for a job. The owner offered to watch his act.

Roberto climbed to the top of the center pole in the great circus tent and with no protection whatsoever, he leaped. He threw out his arms and glided. Then he flapped his arms and rose to the top of the tent. After a summersault, he soared downward, picking up speed. At the very last second, Roberto bent his back and just missed the ground. Flapping like mad, again he rose to the heights of the tent top. As a finish, he did three precision summersaults and gently landed just in front of the circus owner.

Panting to catch his breath, Roberto said, "Well sir, can I have a job?"

"Why would I give you a job?" the owner spat? "No one comes to the circus to see bird imitations."

500. ☆ ☆ ☆ ☆ ☆ ☆ ☆ ☆ ☆

Sometimes a joke can have two or more good endings. You have to pick the version you tell based on the group you are telling the joke to. But remember, you can never tell both jokes to the same group.

Version one:

My Uncle Sol was sitting on the park bench enjoying the nice fall weather when my Uncle Morty came over and joined him. After a few minutes Uncle Morty let out a long anguished sigh.

"Morty, if you're going to talk about the kids, I'm leaving."

501. ☆ ☆ ☆ ☆ ☆ ☆ ☆ ☆ ☆

Version two:

An old man was sitting on the park bench enjoying the nice fall weather when another old man came over and joined him. After a few minutes the second old man let out a long anguished sigh.

"Mister, if you're going to talk politics, I'm leaving!"

502. ☆ ☆ ☆ ☆ ☆ ☆ ☆ ☆ ☆

It was Captain Jack's time to take his pilot license physical. He was a little concerned because rumors had been circulating around the unit that the physical had gotten harder to pass, especially for veteran pilots.

When all was said and done, the doctor informed him that he was a perfect physical specimen. Next came the psychological component of the exam.

"When was the last time you were with a young lady, if you understand what I am asking?" said the obviously uncomfortable young doctor.

"Let me think," said the pilot, "1950?"

"1950?" said the doctor. "Isn't that a long time to go without?"

The pilot thought for a moment as he glanced at his watch, "I don't think so, it's only eleven-hundred hours now."

503. ☆ ☆ ☆ ☆ ☆ ☆ ☆ ☆ ☆

Jesus came upon an angry crowd stoning a young woman accused of adultery. He raised his hands and the crowd quickly calmed.

"May yea among us who hath no sin, throw the first stone," Jesus admonished as he gently helped the broken woman up off the ground.

Suddenly a stone flew by Jesus's ear and struck the woman.

Jesus swung around, peered into the crowd and yelled, "Mom! I wasn't talking to you!"

504.   ☆ ☆ ☆ ☆ ☆ ☆ ☆ ☆ ☆

Walking by a stately home, a hobo meets an attorney who is pruning his roses.

The hobo asks the attorney for a job.

"Are you a God fearing man?" the attorney asks.

"I could be better on account I do tend to drink, but I am an honest hard working man," says the hobo.

The attorney gives the hobo a bucket of paint and a brush. "I'll pay you fairly for painting the porch out back."

About twenty minutes later, the hobo comes back to the attorney, "I painted the Porsche, but it turned out to be a Mercedes."

505.   ☆ ☆ ☆ ☆ ☆ ☆ ☆ ☆ ☆

Mr. Horowitz was feeling a little lonely after he retired, so on the advice of his wife, he decided to get a pet. He went to the local pet store and played with the puppies and kitties but, after days of visiting the store he decided on a parrot. He himself was surprised that he would spend such money on a bird of all things, but he found himself very fond of his new feathered friend, which he named Mr. Bird.

After a few weeks, Mr. Bird was not doing so well. He was listless and barely talking, so Mr. Horowitz took Mr. Bird to the vet. The vet informed him that Mr. Bird was physically fine, but because he was a very intelligent pet he probably missed companionship of his own kind. Especially, female companionship.

Mr. Horowitz was very concerned, so he took Mr. Bird back to the pet store and talked with the owner.

The owner told him that this was very common with intelligent parrots and offered to put Mr. Bird in a cage with a very nice parrot named Polly. It would only cost $50.

"$50," said Mr. Horowitz. "That's a lot of money!"

But just hearing about Polly made Mr. Bird perk right up and start bobbing his head in anticipation. So, Mr. Horowitz forked over the $50.

The pet store owner put Mr. Bird and Polly in the cage together and covered it up with a nice blanket for privacy.

Then all of a sudden, there were screeches. The cage was shaking madly and feathers started to come out from under the blanket.

Pulling back the blanket revealed Mr. Bird holding down Polly by the throat and pulling her feathers out wildly... like a crazed maniac!

"Squark," Mr. Bird screeched, "for 50 bucks I'm seeing you naked!"

506. ☆ ☆ ☆ ☆ ☆ ☆ ☆ ☆ ☆

Howie isn't feeling so good so he calls his brother Marty, the doctor, and asks if he can squeeze him in today. His brother is concerned and tells him to go to the lab and get some blood tests done and he'll see him at noon.

"Well Howie," says Marty. "I got your lab tests back. I have some good news and some bad news."

"Is it serious?" Howie asks.

"The bad news is you only have months to live."

"Oy, what's the good news?" asks Howie.

"You see that gorgeous blond nurse over there with the big boobs? I'm fucking her."

507. ☆ ☆ ☆ ☆ ☆ ☆ ☆ ☆ ☆

Martin got a call from the funeral home that his father's remains had been delivered to them.

"I want to spare no expense, I want my beloved father to get the best funeral, do you understand?" Martin said.

Martin was feeling guilty that he was not going to fly back for his father's funeral, and paying for a grand funeral made him feel better.

When the bill came it was $85,075.84. Martin paid it content with the idea that his father got an appropriate tribute.

The next month another bill came for $75.84. Assuming it was some last minute expense, Martin paid it.

The next month Martin got another bill for $75.84. Curious, he called the funeral home.

"Yes sir, I can explain the bill," the funeral home director said. "You told me you wanted to 'spare no expense' so I rented your father a tux."

508. ☆ ☆ ☆ ☆ ☆ ☆ ☆ ☆ ☆

How do you get a lawyer out of a tree?
Cut the rope.

509. ☆ ☆ ☆ ☆ ☆ ☆ ☆ ☆ ☆

How do you help a lawyer out of the pool?
Take your foot off his head.

510. ☆ ☆ ☆ ☆ ☆ ☆ ☆ ☆ ☆

How many attorneys does it take to grease a manure wagon? Two, but it's best to feed them through slowly.

511. ☆ ☆ ☆ ☆ ☆ ☆ ☆ ☆ ☆

The IRS received an unsigned letter with a new crisp $100 bill inside. The letter read:

```
Dear IRS,

I am a God fearing Christian. Last year I
fibbed a little on my taxes. I have been
unable to sleep because of it. Enclosed
please find $100.

If I still can't sleep, I'll send you the
rest.
```

512. ☆ ☆ ☆ ☆ ☆ ☆ ☆ ☆ ☆

Bumper snicker:

Save a tree... wipe your butt with a spotted owl.

513. ☆ ☆ ☆ ☆ ☆ ☆ ☆ ☆ ☆

Bumper snicker:

Honk if you have never seen an Uzi fired from a car window.

514. ☆ ☆ ☆ ☆ ☆ ☆ ☆ ☆ ☆

A Texan visits a pub in Ireland. He stands on a chair and gives a great hoop-in holler to get everyone's attention. "I hear that you Irish are big drinkers," he yells.

The Irish bar patrons yell and laugh.

"Well" the Texan continues, "I'll bet any man in here 500 America greenbacks that he can't drink ten pints of Guinness, one right after another."

The patrons muttered, but no one takes the bet. One little fellow even ran out of the place.

The Texan laughed and sat on down and enjoyed himself a Guinness in victory.

Fifteen minutes go by and the little fellow who left earlier, comes back into the bar and says, "You wouldn't still be offering that bet, now would you?"

The Texan looks him over and laughs. "Sure little fella, your money's as good as anyone else's. Barkeep, line my friend up ten pints of your finest."

The little Irishman bellies up to the bar. One pint, then two, and in less then a minute he downs all ten! The bar goes wild with excitement.

The Texan laughs the loss off as he pays the $500. "Hey friend, where did you go for fifteen minutes?"

"Well, laddie," the Irishmen said, "First, I popped into the bar down the street to see if I could do it, then I peed for 10 minutes, then I came right back here."

515. ☆ ☆ ☆ ☆ ☆ ☆ ☆ ☆ ☆

Jack came home to find his wife in the arms of his best friend.

"Jack I'm so sorry, it just happened," said Jill, "but I love him."

"Jack," said the best friend, "we need to be mature about this. Sometimes things just happen. How about we play a game of gin rummy and the winner gets to keep Jill."

Jack thought about this for a moment, then said, "Sure, we're both civilized men, but let's play for a penny a point just to keep it interesting."

516. ☆ ☆ ☆ ☆ ☆ ☆ ☆ ☆ ☆

In the old country a lady of the evening was called a 'nafte', the yiddish word for prostitute. The women in the town pretended they didn't know what she did, but behind her back everyone called her

Mrs. Nafkewitz.

When Uncle Morty first came to New York City he didn't know anybody. After a few months he was very homesick and was surprised when he saw Mrs. Nafkewitz across the street. He yelled to her, "Mrs. Nafkewitz, Mrs. Nafkewitz!"

She crossed the street to shush Uncle Monty, "Don't say that! Here they call me Mrs. Horowitz."

"Oh ... I motivate the kids by waking them up early and telling them that they can't pee until their chores are all done."

517. ☆ ☆ ☆ ☆ ☆ ☆ ☆ ☆ ☆

Aunt Sadie picked up her daughter from Sunday school. "So what did you learn today, Hanna?"

"We learned about Moses."

"Moses, good." said Aunt Sadie. "What did you learn about Moses?"

"We learned that Moses was on a long holiday in Egypt. When it was time to go, Moses got all his friends to pack up and go. This made the Pharaoh very angry. It got scary and the Jews had to get out fast! So they ran and the Pharaoh's army chased them. The Jews were taking casualties, but luckily the Pharaoh's army was bogged down because of their heavy tanks in the desert sand. Moses and his people got backed up against the Red Sea so, Moses called in air support…"

"What!" said Aunt Sadie all flustered. "That's what the teacher told you?"

"Not exactly," said Hanna. "But if I told you the story she told us… you'd never believe it!"

518. ☆☆☆☆☆☆☆☆☆☆

Seen on the back of a biker's jacket: If you can read this, the bitch fell off.

When telling a joke, it is important to keep in mind your audience. A well told joke with one group, won't go over so well with another. Unfortunately, often this is a lesson that we have to learn the hard way.

Here is another example of how to use the same joke for different occasions:

519. ☆☆☆☆☆☆☆☆☆☆

Version one:

A prisoner was condemned to death by firing squad. The warden roused him at four A.M. and had him shackled and marched out into the cold and rainy morning. He was stood in front of the designated wall and blindfolded.

"Any last words?" barked the warden.

"Yes," said the prisoner. "It is barbaric to have me marched out here in this weather just to be shot."

"What are you complaining about?" said the warden. "We also have to march back!"

520. ☆☆☆☆☆☆☆☆☆☆

Version two:

Mr. Martin Cohen is told the devastating news by his doctor, "You have one day to live."

As you can imagine, all he want is to be with his beloved wife Greta. They hold each other, they cry together, they tell lovely stories of their happy 22 year marriage.

At bedtime Martin cuddles up to Greta. "My little cupcake," he says. You know what I want to do for my last night on earth? I want to make passionate love to you. I want to kiss you all over. I want to bring you such pleasures..."

"That's nice for you Marty," Greta interrupts. "But I gotta get up in the morning."

521. ☆ ☆ ☆ ☆ ☆ ☆ ☆ ☆ ☆

Uncle Sol was running late for work when he got pulled over by a cop. The cop approached the car and asked Uncle Sol for his license and registration.

"What do you want to do that for? You want to give me a ticket?" said Uncle Sol.

"Sir its the law..."

"But I was in a hurry, I'm late for work," said Uncle Sol.

"What do you do that is so important that you think it is OK for you to speed?" The cop asked.

"I'm a rectum stretcher at Mount Sinai Hospital."

"What? I never heard of such a thing," said the cop.

"Well it's true, I stretch rectums in the surgery. It's a very important job," explained Uncle Sol.

"What?" says the cop in disbelief.

"You know, I stretch rectums. I put in a finger, then more fingers, then my fist, and I stretch. Then two fists and I stretch. I stretch until the rectum is six feet wide," said Uncle Sol.

"Really?" asks the cop. "What would anybody do with a six foot asshole?"

"Sometimes they hide them under the overpass and give them a radar gun."

522. ☆ ☆ ☆ ☆ ☆ ☆ ☆ ☆ ☆

An old Jewish man starts up a conversation with a hooker in a hotel bar in Las Vegas.

The topic quickly turns to money and the old man asks what he can get for twenty dollars.

"Twenty dollars," says the hooker, "you can't get anything for twenty dollars. It costs $200 just to get me to come up to your room."

So, the old man leaves.

The next morning the old man is checking out with his wife and that same hooker comes up to him and says, "You see... that's what you get for twenty dollars."

523.   ☆ ☆ ☆ ☆ ☆ ☆ ☆ ☆ ☆

A letter to a congressman:

Dear Sir,

I have been at boot camp for one week now, and I would like to complain about how I am being treated in this here army. The sergeant yells at me constantly, he wakes me up at 4 o'clock in the morning just to make me carry a heavy pack around for his amusement.

The worst thing is the food! I wouldn't feed it to my hogs back home for fear it would bloat their stomachs and cause them a horrifyingly painful death. On top of all that, you can only get one small helping!

524.   ☆ ☆ ☆ ☆ ☆ ☆ ☆ ☆ ☆

A lady consulted a psychiatrist because she was concern for the sanity of her husband.

"You see Dr. Finkelstein, for two years my husband has thought he was a chicken."

"That sounds very serious," said Dr. Finkelstein. "But why did you wait so long to get help?"

"Well, I kind of like the fresh eggs every morning."

525.   ☆ ☆ ☆ ☆ ☆ ☆ ☆ ☆ ☆

It was amazing, Mrs. Levi was 88 years old and gave birth to a healthily baby boy. You probably heard about it. It was in all the newspapers. My Aunt Sadie went over to see the new baby. When she got to her friend's apartment, Mrs. Levi looked a little tuckered out.

"Ruth you look terrible," Aunt Sadie said, "I came over to help. I'll watch the baby while you take a nap."

"Na. It's OK I got everything under control. Do you want some coffee or a nice piece of whitefish?" asked Ruth Levi.

"Whitefish, what whitefish? I want to see the baby."

"First you should sit and relax," said Ruth, "I'll make you an iced tea."

"Sit! What do you mean sit? I took two subway trains and a bus to get here. I want to see the baby."

"Sure," said Ruth. "I'll show you the baby when he cries."

"Stop playing around, I want to see the little bubala," yelled Aunt Sadie.

"To tell you the truth," said Ruth, "you'll have to wait until he cries, I forgot where I put him."

Even on the worst of rainy days, Mary Haspirin, psychotherapist multitasks by doing her Kegels.

526. ☆ ☆ ☆ ☆ ☆ ☆ ☆ ☆ ☆ ☆

Did you hear that Jesus walked into a bar and ordered a wine glass filled with water?

527.   ☆ ☆ ☆ ☆ ☆ ☆ ☆ ☆ ☆

The police officer pulled over a vintage Cadillac for going 22 on the highway. He was surprise to find four little old ladies in the car. The driver looked fine, but the other three looked scared to death.

"Ma'am," the officer said, I pulled you over for going 22 in a 55 zone."

"I assure you sonny," the driver said. "I was doing the speed limit, the sign read 22."

"Twenty-two is the highway number, not the speed limit," said the officer. "Are your passengers alright?"

"I'm sure they will be," the kindly old driver said, "I'm guessing we just got off Highway 120."

528.   ☆ ☆ ☆ ☆ ☆ ☆ ☆ ☆ ☆

Mr. Moskowitz went to his doctor and told him that he had been feeling lousy for a few weeks. The doctor ran all the tests and reported the bad news to him.

"Mr. Moskowitz, my old friend, there is no way I can say this that will make you feel any better. Unfortunately, you only have a few months to live."

"Oy," said Mr. Moskowitz. "What should I do?"

"Maybe you should go to the famous healing mud baths at Saint Lucia," said his friend the doctor.

"Is that going to help?"

"Not really," said the doctor, "but it will help you to get used to dirt."

529.   ☆ ☆ ☆ ☆ ☆ ☆ ☆ ☆ ☆

Mr. Moskowitz returns a few months later to see his friend the doctor. "I'm not feeling any better, in fact I'm feeling worse. What do my lab tests say?"

"It's not good," says the doctor.

"Not good, what's with not good?" asks Mr. Moskowitz.

"Ten now maybe 9..."

"Ten maybe 9 what, what do the tests say, stop playing around, this isn't funny," says Mr. Moskowitz.

"Six…"
"Six what, what's with the six?"
"Five… four… three…"

530. ☆☆☆☆☆☆☆☆☆

The patient tells her doctor, "Every time I sneeze I have an orgasm."

"Interesting medical condition," says the doctor. "Have you taken anything for it?"

"Sure, I find pepper helps."

531. ☆☆☆☆☆☆☆☆☆

My Aunt Sadie took her beloved dog to the vet for its annual check-up. The vet said the dog was doing great except that he should lose a few pounds, and that Aunt Sadie should keep the hair out of his ear canal by using a hair removal foam in his ears once a month.

Not knowing much about hair removal foam, Aunt Sadie asked the old pharmacist down at Weinstein's Pharmacy.

"If you're using it on your legs you shouldn't shave for a week," said the pharmacist.

"It's not for my legs," said Aunt Sadie.

"Well if you're using it for your underarms you shouldn't shave their either for a week," said the pharmacist.

"It's not for my armpits, it's for my Schnauzer."

"Well on that account," explained the pharmacist, "don't ride a bike for at least a week."

532. ☆☆☆☆☆☆☆☆☆

"Doc, I feel terrible, my throat hurts, my head is pounding and I ache all over," the patient says.

"Let me take a look here," the doctor says looking at the patent's sore throat, "How long has this been going on?"

"A few days, everyone in the office is sick, will I be OK?"

"Sure," smiled the doctor. "You have a common staff infection."

533. ☆ ☆ ☆ ☆ ☆ ☆ ☆ ☆ ☆

Katie knew something really bad happened when the priest and the manager of the Guinness brewery came walking up the front walk.

"Katie, can we come in?" said Father O'Mallery.

"There has been a terrible accident down at the plant. Your husband drowned after he fell into a vat," the manager said.

"Was it quick, please God tell me he didn't suffer," Katie said through tears.

"Unfortunately, it took hours," said the priest. "The poor soul only had the strength to get out three times to pee."

534. ☆ ☆ ☆ ☆ ☆ ☆ ☆ ☆ ☆

Rabbi Cohen called on old Mr. Moskowitz to help with a problem. The temple's roof had sprung a leak and there was need for some emergency money from the congregation. Sixteen-thousand dollars was needed right away.

"OK, OK," Mr. Moskowitz said to the rabbi. "But it will be hard. We just had our annual fundraiser last month. If you want me to get donations, I've got to do it my way. No interference Rabbi, do you understand?"

"You have my total support," said the rabbi. "Please go forth and fleece my flock."

A few hours later Mr. Moskowitz knocked on the rabbi's door. When he was invited in, he placed 2 grocery bags on the rabbi's desk. The large one was brimming with cash. The smaller one was rolled down neatly from the top.

"Here's the $17,000 you needed. I got a little extra just in case," Mr. Moskowitz said.

The rabbi was amazed. "You were able to get such money in just a few hours? How did you do it?"

"It was easy," said Mr. Moskowitz. "I stood by the urinals in the main bathroom. When a man was relieving himself I showed him my little pen knife and said, "Do you mind donating to the emergency roof fund? If you don't feel like it, the rabbi said I can redo your bris.'[11] In no time, I had the money you needed.'"

The rabbi was in shock, "But, but... what's with the little bag?"

Mr. Moskowitz pushed the little bag closer to the rabbi and said, "You know, not everybody gives."

535. ☆ ☆ ☆ ☆ ☆ ☆ ☆ ☆ ☆

Did you hear about the cat that killed the German Shepherd?
It crawled into it's throat and choked it to death. It was a suicide mission.

536. ☆ ☆ ☆ ☆ ☆ ☆ ☆ ☆ ☆

"I grew up an atheist," Sarah told her therapist. "As a young child I hated it. No holidays. One birthday my parents gave me a Cabbage Patch doll filled with cat nip. They told me it was a Christian and I should introduce it to my cat.

"It didn't get better when I got older. Now when I have an orgasm, I have no one to call out thanks to.

"One time I accidentally yelled out, 'OH, thank you Charles Darwin... oh Charlie, oh Charlie!' That date ended abruptly."

537. ☆ ☆ ☆ ☆ ☆ ☆ ☆ ☆ ☆

According to Erma Bombeck, "Never lend your car to anyone to whom you have given birth."

538. ☆ ☆ ☆ ☆ ☆ ☆ ☆ ☆ ☆

I tell the following joke to doctor groups. It always gets a huge laugh.

At the Pearly Gates, St. Peter asked the dignified looking man what his major accomplishments were in life.

"For the last 30 years I ran Blue Cross. I quadrupled its earnings and paid dividends to its stockholders far above market expectations."

---

[11] The Jewish ceremony of circumcision.

St. Peter did not look impressed. He went to a shelf of books and poured over them. He made calculations and a few graphs.

"After consulting the data," St. Peter explained. "I have determined that you can come into Heaven for 3 days, then you can go to hell!"

539. ☆ ☆ ☆ ☆ ☆ ☆ ☆ ☆

Three Jewish women were having lunch when the conversation turned to, "If you could sleep with anybody, who would you invite into your bed?"

Becky said, "I'd pick George Clooney, now that's a real man."

Then Silvia said, "Clooney is definitely a looker, but I'd have to go with Michael Caine. He's handsome, and what an accent!"

"Me," said Hilda, "I'd have to chose my husband's partner."

"What are you talking about," laughed Silvia. "Why would you pick Bernie over George Clooney or Michael Caine?"

"Because whenever my husband talks about his partner he always says, 'What a schmuck, what a big schmuck!"

"The Pope recently told me that I shouldn't name drop, but I was talking to Paul McCartney and he said..."

540. ☆☆☆☆☆☆☆☆☆

Bernie comes home and is surprised to find his wife sitting on the bed totally nude and rubbing her breast with a silk hanky.

"Rachel honey," Bernie says. "What are you doing?"

"I read in a magazine that if you rub silk on your breast a little bit every day they will grow," Rachel said. "Do you think it's true?"

"I don't know about silk, why don't you try toilet paper?"

"Toilet paper?" asks Rachel.

"I guess," said Bernie, "look what it's done for your ass."

541. ☆☆☆☆☆☆☆☆☆

After the funeral the kids find their mother in the kitchen. The oldest boy says, "Mama, you and Papa were together for 60 years. Today of all days, you shouldn't be cooking for us. Let us take care of you."

"I'm not cooking for you, I'm doing this for me," Mama says angrily.

Then the oldest boy realizes what mama is frying in the skillet. "Is that what I think it is… is that's papa's you know what?"

"That's right," mama says, "for 60 years he wanted it his way."

542. ☆☆☆☆☆☆☆☆☆

Mr. Rubinstein goes to the doctor and asks for Viagra. "Doc, I'm going to need some for Friday night because my wife is out of town for the weekend and my lady friend is coming over. I'll also need some for Saturday night, my mistress is coming over. And Sunday night too. I don't want my wife to get suspicious when she gets home."

"Mr. Rubinstein that's a lot of Viagra for a man of your age," says the doctor. "I'll give you the prescription, but I want to see you Monday to make sure you're OK."

First thing Monday morning Mr. Rubinstein walks into the doctor's office wearing a sling on both arms.

"What happened?" asked the doctor.

"No one showed!"

543. ☆ ☆ ☆ ☆ ☆ ☆ ☆ ☆ ☆

Mr. Moskowitz died and went to heaven. St. Peter was pleased to see him and invited him in.

"I've always been curious what hell was like, am I allowed to visit?" Mr. Moskowitz asked.

"It is a little unorthodox, but why not, I'll let you," said St. Peter.

And with that, Mr. Moskowitz was at the cave opening to hell. He watched as Satan walked up to the people in line and pinched them. Most he tossed into a fiery hole. But some he piled up off to the side. Curious, Mr. Moskowitz asked Satan what he was doing.

"Most go directly into the fires of Hades," explained Satan, "but this lot is from Seattle so they're too wet to burn for a few months."

544. ☆ ☆ ☆ ☆ ☆ ☆ ☆ ☆ ☆

A young Australian sailor was very excited to finally make it to the big city of San Francisco. As soon as he got shore leave he found himself a pretty prostitute and rented a room for the night.

As the lady started to undress, the Aussie sailor began rearranging the room. He pushed the bed into the middle and all the furniture to one corner. Then he started to throw whatever wasn't nailed down out the window.

The lady was getting nervous, "What are you planning to do to me sailor?" she asked.

"I'm not quite sure, Ma'am," he smiled broadly, "but if it's anything like being with a kangaroo, we're gonna need lots of room."

545. ☆ ☆ ☆ ☆ ☆ ☆ ☆ ☆ ☆

A Texan walked into a bar and yelled, "My wife just had a 20 pound baby boy, all drinks are on me!"

About a week later the Texan comes back into the bar and the bartender says, "That sure was grand of you to buy a round for everyone last week, how is that boy of yours doing?"

"Ah, he's a great baby, a real son of Texas!"

"How much does he weigh now?" asked the barkeep.

"We just had him weighed this morning. He weighs 12 pounds 4 ounces."

"Twelve pounds, is he OK?" asked the barkeep. "How come he lost so much weight?"

"Had him circumcised."

546. ☆ ☆ ☆ ☆ ☆ ☆ ☆ ☆ ☆

The ladies at the country club are bragging about their children.

"My Timothy is a Bishop now. When he walks into a room people say, 'Your Worship,' and politely bow."

"When my son the Cardinal walks into a room they say, 'Your Holiness,' and then kneel and kiss his ring."

"Mrs. Rosenbaum, I hear you don't have any sons," one of the ladies says.

"This is true," states Mrs. Rosenbaum, "When my Becky walks into a room they look at how beautiful she is and whisper, 'Oh my god!'"

547. ☆ ☆ ☆ ☆ ☆ ☆ ☆ ☆ ☆

Mrs. Anderson was a kind Christian woman who was getting on in years and feeling a little lonely. So she decided to get a parrot to have someone to talk to in the apartment.

She went to the pet store and inquired about a parrot.

"I'm sorry ma'am, I only have one parrot and he used to be owned by a sailor. He's got a really foul mouth on him, you don't want that."

"That sounds interesting," said Mrs. Anderson. "Maybe I could reform his wayward behavior and bring him back to the Lord."

So she bought the foul mouthed parrot and took him home. As soon as the parrot was placed in his cage he looked around and said, "Nice God damn apartment, squark!"

"We'll have none of that salty talk. This is your only warning." Mrs. Anderson said. "Nasty talk gets you a time out."

"Time out! I don't give a shit about time out, squark!" said the parrot.

Mrs. Anderson was very upset and said. "OK, you will learn, you have a five minute time out."

With that she grabbed the bird and marched into the kitchen and stuffed him into the freezer.

After five minutes, she took the parrot out of the freezer and said, "Have you learned your lesson?"

"Yes ma'am, I no use bad words," said the parrot.

"Very well," Mrs. Anderson smiled.

"Just one question, ma'am, if you don't mind," asked the parrot, "What the fuck did the turkey do?"

548.   ☆ ☆ ☆ ☆ ☆ ☆ ☆ ☆

Ettie was no spring chicken when she married Marvin. At the the bridal suite Ettie confesses, "Marvin I love you so you should know, I'm still a virgin."

"Ettie," Marvin laughs, "what are you talking about. You've been married three times already."

"Marvin you don't understand," Ettie says as she sits on the bed, nervously twisting the handkerchief in her hands. "My first husband, Milton, was a psychiatrist, all he wanted to do was talk to it. My second husband, Norm was a gynecologist, all he wanted to do was look at it. My third husband, Bernie was a stamp collector all he wanted to do is... Oy, do I miss Bernie!"

"That's interesting, Ettie," said Marvin. "I'm an attorney, you know it's my nature to screw you!"

549. ☆☆☆☆☆☆☆☆☆

It is a brisk January morning in the nation's capital and thousands of people are in attendance for the historic inauguration of the first Jewish-American president. Her mother is sitting in attendance between a four star general and a supreme court justice.

The proud mother taps the general on in the sleeve, "That's my youngest daughter over there, isn't she beautiful? Did you know her brother's a doctor. He's a good boy, he's on staff at Mount Sinai."

550. ☆☆☆☆☆☆☆☆☆

Winston Churchill once angered a woman at a party. She snapped at him, "'Mr. Churchill, if you were my husband, I'd poison your tea!"

Churchill replied, "If you were my wife, I would drink it!"

551. ☆☆☆☆☆☆☆☆☆

Bessie Braddock, was a British Labor politician. I think this story is erroneous but I still like it, so I am including it.

"'You are drunk Sir Winston, you are disgustingly drunk."

"Yes, Mrs. Braddock, I am drunk. But you, Mrs. Braddock are ugly, and disgustingly fat. But, tomorrow morning, I, Winston Churchill will be sober."

552. ☆☆☆☆☆☆☆☆☆

Winston Churchill was known for taking long, very hot baths. During World War II he regularly had meetings with his ministers or staff officers while he bathed. He did not seem to be a modest man. People that attended such meetings were called "Companions of the Bath." When Brigadier Menzies, chief of the British Secret Service was asked about the bath meetings, he said that "Prime Minister Churchill looked like a nice pink pig wrapped in a silk kimono." Of the bath stories, this is my favorite:

Once in the White House, President Roosevelt came into Churchill's room as he was emerging from his customary hot bath. Churchill stood naked and red from the hot water. Churchill said, "You see the Prime Minster of Great Britain has nothing to hide from the President of the United States."

"Yes! This year's eye slits <u>are very</u> slimming."

553. ☆ ☆ ☆ ☆ ☆ ☆ ☆ ☆ ☆

Mr. Grievous was telling his wife about the rough day he had down at the mortuary.

"We had two very large showings today and Robert and Carl were out sick. I accidentally dressed the departed in the wrong suits and didn't notice until just minutes before the unveilings."

"You should have called," Mrs. Grievous said. "I would have come right over and helped."

"There wasn't time, so I just switched the heads."

554. ☆ ☆ ☆ ☆ ☆ ☆ ☆ ☆ ☆

"I'm not sure what is really going on with you," the doctor tells his patient, "I think it could be caused by heavy drinking."

"I understand, Doc," says the patient. "Why don't I come back when you're sober?"

555. ☆ ☆ ☆ ☆ ☆ ☆ ☆ ☆ ☆

A nervous middle aged man knocked on the farmhouse door. Little Suzy May answered the door and smiled, "If you're here about the bull, he's $250. He's guaranteed and certified."

"No little girl," the man said, "I need to see your father."

"If that's too much, we got another bull for $150 he's guaranteed but has no papers."

"No young lady," said the man, "I really need to talk to your father."

"We also got a $100 bull, but he's got no papers and he ain't guaranteed," continued Suzy May.

"No little missy, I insist on talking to your father about Elmer, he got my Sally pregnant!" the nervous man exclaimed.

"You're gonna have to talk to Pa about my brother, I don't know what he charges for Elmer."

556. ☆ ☆ ☆ ☆ ☆ ☆ ☆ ☆ ☆

Mr. Mendelson is turning 90 so he has a physical to please his wife. After all the tests are done, the doctor meets with Mr. and Mrs. Mendelson and says, "Mr. Mendelson you are in remarkably good heath. My only concern is on the Life Questionnaire you completed you stated that the first time you have sex you feel great, but the second time you break out in a sweat and are totally drenched. What do you think is causing this?"

"I can tell you doctor," says Mrs. Mendelson. "The first time is in January and the second time is in July."

557. ☆ ☆ ☆ ☆ ☆ ☆ ☆ ☆ ☆

Marvin Shlemeil goes to the doctor. The doctory says, "I don't know how to say this, but you have to stop masturbating."

"Why?"

"So I can examine you!"

"I was so upset that I told my congregation that I was 'fit to be tithed!'"

558. ☆ ☆ ☆ ☆ ☆ ☆ ☆ ☆ ☆

After the medical exam, Marvin Shlemeil asks the doctor, "Do you think I'm a hypochondriac?"

"I'm not a psychiatrist so I'm not really sure," said the doctor. "But in 30 years of being a gynecologist, you're the first man I've examined."

559. ☆ ☆ ☆ ☆ ☆ ☆ ☆ ☆ ☆

A Frenchman, a German and my Uncle Monty were lost in the desert.

The Frenchman said, "I'm tired, I'm thirsty, I must have wine."

The German said, "I'm tired, I'm thirsty, I must have beer."

And Uncle Monty said, "Oy vey[12], I'm tired, I'm thirsty, I must have diabetes."

560. ☆ ☆ ☆ ☆ ☆ ☆ ☆ ☆ ☆

Mark and Susie were getting very serious about each other. So, Susie suggested that Mark meet her parents.

"I don't know, meeting the parents is kind of scary," Mark confessed.

Susie expected this so she was ready, "You know I won't sleep with anybody that has not made a good impression on my parents."

The next morning, thinking it was a good idea to be prepared, Mark went to the pharmacy to get some condoms.

While ringing up the order, the pharmacist chitchatted, "You seem very happy today."

"Well, I am sir... I think that tonight I'm going to get lucky with my girlfriend," Mark smiled. "She is beautiful, and I think a virgin. I think tonight is the night."

That night, as Mark walked to the door of Susie's home he was nervous. He rang the bell and Susie's father opened the door, "Welcome, you must be Susie's boyfriend?"

Mark suddenly knelt down, put his palms together and started to pray. "Oh, heavenly father..."

Susie rushed by her father and dragged her boyfriend to his feet, "I didn't know you were so religious," she snapped.

Looking sick to his stomach Mark said, "I didn't know your father was a pharmacist!"

---

[12] Yiddish: short for "Oy vey iz mir," Oh, woe is me!

561. ☆ ☆ ☆ ☆ ☆ ☆ ☆ ☆ ☆

"Why do they call the new girl Cinderella?" asked one executive to another.

"Oh, she's lovely," he explained, "and at midnight she turns into a motel.

562. ☆ ☆ ☆ ☆ ☆ ☆ ☆ ☆ ☆

Every week, week after week, a homely looking old man comes

into Sussmann's Pharmacy and buys two dozen condoms. Mr. Sussmann's curiosity gets the better of him so he asks, "I'm not one to judge, but what's with all the condoms?"

"I feed them to my poodle," said the old man. "This way she poops in little plastic bags."

563. ☆ ☆ ☆ ☆ ☆ ☆ ☆ ☆ ☆ ☆

Did you hear that the Minnesota Vikings place kicker attempted suicide?

He stood on a bucket and put a noose around his neck. It turned out OK because he wasn't able to kick the bucket out from under himself.

564. ☆ ☆ ☆ ☆ ☆ ☆ ☆ ☆ ☆ ☆

Sheldon is visiting his mother in the Bronx.

"Ma, I just met the super in the elevator. He's a rude and crude man," said Sheldon.

"Really? He has always been kind to me."

"I don't like him," said Sheldon. "He just told me that every woman in this building, except one, has given him oral sex."

"Really," said Sheldon's mother, "I bet it's that skinny Irish woman down in 7B."

565. ☆ ☆ ☆ ☆ ☆ ☆ ☆ ☆ ☆ ☆

Marcus was sitting in a small bar nursing a beer. The man at the far end of the counter got up and walked to the back wall. He then proceeded to crawl up the wall and across the ceiling. When he got to the front wall of the place, he did a summersault and landed softly on his feet. After brushing off the knees of his pants, he walked out the door.

Marcus looked at the bartender and said, "That was odd, wasn't it?"

"Not really," the barkeep said, "he always leaves without saying goodbye."

566. ☆ ☆ ☆ ☆ ☆ ☆ ☆ ☆ ☆

Abe and Rachel are having a big argument about money. It's always about money.

"If you think it is so easy to make money," Abe yells, "go out and get a job!"

"I can't get a job I'm seventy-two years old, I know nothing… what can I do?" Rachel says.

"It doesn't matter," growls Abe. "You can work the streets for all I care!"

Rachel is so angry with Abe, she snaps, "Alright, I'll be a common prostitute if that's what you want! I'll make my own money!"

Then she grabs her coat and leaves, slamming the door in all her fury.

Hours go by and Rachel doesn't return. Abe is starting to worry about her. So he decides to go find her. Just then the apartment door opens and Rachel is there all disheveled. Her housedress is ripped and her brassiere is showing. It looks ripped too. Her hair is a mess and her glasses are hanging from one ear.

"I did it, I made $32.10!" Rachel said with a wheeze.

"$32.10? Abe repeated. "Who paid you 10¢?"

"They all did."

567. ☆ ☆ ☆ ☆ ☆ ☆ ☆ ☆ ☆

Archeologists in Israel found a wall deep under the sands of time with unusual art depicted on it. The section of the wall was carefully removed and taken to the National Museum. For two years scholars speculated and argued over its meanings. Carbon dating indicated that the symbols were older, by thousands of years, than others found in the surrounding areas.

Finally an international conference was held to unveil the consensus of the researchers. The president of the committee delivered the keynote speech.

"The committee has determined that the symbols show that the people that created this artifact had understanding unusual for the time. For example, the first symbol looks like a tomato. This indicates the ability of these people to cultivate and harvest food.

"The second symbol looks like a donkey, indicating animal husbandry. The third symbol looks like a spade probably indicative of advanced tool making well ahead of its time. The fourth symbol looks like a fish, indicating their ability to harvest food from the sea. The last symbol looks like the Star of David indicating organized religion."

"I don't think so," came a voice from the back of the room.

"What, you disagree with our findings?" the committee president asks. "What institution do you represent?"

"I'm not with nobody. I'm Herby Goldblatt, a CPA from the Bronx. I just sat down while my wife went to the ladies."

"Well thank you sir, but…"

"I don't want to meddle," Herby interrupted, "but I think you are reading it backwards. I think it reads, 'Holy mackerel, dig the ass on that tomato.'"

568. ☆ ☆ ☆ ☆ ☆ ☆ ☆ ☆ ☆

A man walked into a bar with a small monkey on his shoulder. Within seconds the hyperactive monkey was terrorizing the place. He was jumping from table to table eating and drinking anything and everything he could get his paws onto.

At one point, the monkey got onto the pool table and swallowed the cue ball whole. The monkey's owner grabbed the monkey. On the way out he dropped a hundred dollar bill on the counter, apologized, then left.

A few weeks later, the same man came into the bar with the monkey on a leash. The monkey jumped off his shoulder and helped himself to some peanuts.

The bartender was watching the monkey as he took each peanut and stuck it up his butt. Then he ate it.

"Hey, what's that weird monkey doing now?" asked the bartender.

"Oh," said the man, "ever since the cue ball, he checks to make sure it fits before he eats anything."

569.   ☆ ☆ ☆ ☆ ☆ ☆ ☆ ☆ ☆

Joe and Barney were pushing their large wheelbarrows alongside the parade. Barney turned to Joe and complained. "I'm tired of picking up manure all day. The horse poop really smells and the elephant poop is really heavy."

"Yeah, but what are you going to do?" agreed Joe.

"I also hate that it is hard to get a date, no matter how much I scrub, I can't get the stink off!"

"Yeah, but what are you going to do?" agreed Joe.

"I've been thinking about quitting!"

"Quit!" screamed Joe. "And get out of show business?"

570.   ☆ ☆ ☆ ☆ ☆ ☆ ☆ ☆ ☆

The government man ask the small boy, "Where is your daddy?"

"Up at the still," said the boy.

"I'll give you a dollar if you tell me where your father's still is," said the man.

"Sure, but you have to give me the dollar first."

"No son, I'll give you the dollar when I come back," said the government man.

"No thanks mister," smiled the boy. "If I know my pappy, you ain't coming back."

571.   ☆ ☆ ☆ ☆ ☆ ☆ ☆ ☆ ☆

A man walked into a bar and found the barkeep playing chess with a schnauzer. As the man watched, the schnauzer carefully moved his knight and barked softly to indicate "check."

"That's one smart dog," the man said.

"Not really," said the bartender, "I've won three of the last four games."

What's nice about a joke like this, you can tell it to a friend about their favorite dog breed. If no breed matters to your audience, you should pick a funnier sounding breed such as schnauzer, wiener dog, or yappi-doodle. Some words are inherently funnier than others. Bull mastiff is not funny while labadoole is. I have told this joke a few times to cat peo-

ple, but the joke kind of fell flat. I think it's because cat people know no cat would lower itself to play a simple board game.

572.   ☆ ☆ ☆ ☆ ☆ ☆ ☆ ☆ ☆

Walter went into a small bar to find only the barkeeper reading the paper and a dog and cat sleeping on the floor.

After a few minutes, the dog stood up slowly, enjoyed a long dog stretch followed by a huge yawn, then he said, "See you later Ted," as he walked out the door.

Walter couldn't believe what he thought he just witnessed and said to the barkeep, "Did you hear that dog?"

"Don't be silly," said the barkeep. "Dogs can't talk."

"But, I just heard it. Honest!"

"I tell you dogs are dumb, they can't talk... it was that wiseass cat... he's a ventriloquist."

Cat people love this joke.

573.   ☆ ☆ ☆ ☆ ☆ ☆ ☆ ☆ ☆

While driving though central New York state, two guys from California come across the Tioughnioga River. Never having heard the name before they tried to figure out how to pronounce it. Was it ti-af-ne-o-ga or is it tee-uf-ne-o-guh?

They decided to stop at a burger place for lunch and one of the guys said to the server, "Could you carefully pronounce the name of this place? My friend and I are curious.

"Sure, I guess," said the girl, "buuur-geeer-kiiing."

574.   ☆ ☆ ☆ ☆ ☆ ☆ ☆ ☆ ☆

A nun comes running out of the doctor's examining room in tears. Concerned, the nurse goes up to the doctor, "Is everything OK with Sister Clara?"

"I had to tell her she was pregnant," said the doctor.

"Oh my," whispered the nurse, "she's pregnant?"

"No, but I sure cured her hiccups."

575. ☆ ☆ ☆ ☆ ☆ ☆ ☆ ☆ ☆ ☆

An attractive young lady was walking down a city street. As she turned the corner the wind almost blew her hat off. Holding her hat with both hands she noticed two gentleman happily watching her dress billow up. Being the sophisticated young woman she was, she politely addressed the gents, "What you're enjoying I've had for 23 years, this hat I just bought."

576. ☆ ☆ ☆ ☆ ☆ ☆ ☆ ☆ ☆

Billy Bob from Arkansas went to the big city and stayed in a hotel for the first time. In the morning he called the front desk because he couldn't figure out how to get out of his room.

"Sir, use the door," said the man at the front desk.

"I tried that," said Billy Bob. "One leads to the bathroom, one goes to the closet, and the other one has a 'do not disturb' sign on it."

577. ☆ ☆ ☆ ☆ ☆ ☆ ☆ ☆ ☆

After watching, Who Wants To Be a Millionaire, Harold turns to Maude and asks, "Do you want to make a little woopti-doopti?"

"Not tonight Harold, I'm tired."

"Is that your final answer?"

"Yes!"

"Well then," Harold says, "I'd like to call a friend."

578. ☆ ☆ ☆ ☆ ☆ ☆ ☆ ☆ ☆

Bubbe[13] came to pick up her 3-year old grandson and take him to the beach.

"Now momma, make sure he doesn't get hurt," the overly protective mother said to Bubbe. "It's cold outside, make sure he stays warm."

"I raised 7 children without your help young lady," Bubbe reminded her daughter. "When I need information about how to raise children, I'll be sure to call you."

"But momma, it's cold outside, make sure he keeps his coat and hat on."

"I know, I know, who do you think taught you such important things?" Bubbe said.

While walking along the shore, Bubbe made sure that her perfect grandchild was bundled warm, for it was 55 degrees outside and, as you probably know, you can catch a death of cold if you're at the beach any day that is below 96 degrees!

All of a sudden, a rogue wave came up onto the beach and washed the grandchild out to sea. Bubbe was beside herself. She ran knee deep into the ocean and yelled furiously at God.

"HOW DARE YOU LET THIS HAPPEN TO MY GRAND-BABY! BRING HIM BACK TO ME THIS INSTANT!"

And like a miracle, another rouge wave washed the small boy back onto the beach. The grandmother rushed to him, and throwing herself to her knees she hugged the child and checked him from head

---

[13] Yiddish for grandmother

to toe. He was completely unharmed.

Bubbe picked the child up in one arm and with a powerful fist she punched angrily high into the air screaming, "HE HAD A HAT!"

579. ☆ ☆ ☆ ☆ ☆ ☆ ☆ ☆ ☆

Marcus and Levi are devastated to hear that their partner died. To help with their grief, they decide to get new suits made by Pincus the tailor.

"Pincus, we need the blackest of black material for the funeral. We have to have the blackest of black to show our grief," Marcus explained.

"I have exactly what you need," assured Pincus. "I will stay up all night if I have to. You will have the perfect suits,".

"They have to be as black as our sorrow!" says Levi.

"I understand, this material is as black as it comes, I special order it specifically for nuns' habits. It's black I tell you."

The morning of the funeral, Marcus and Levi pick up their new suits from Pincus and are happy with the fit. Once on the street, Marcus says, "I hope these suits are as black as possible."

Levi sees two nuns walking up the street. "I'm going to see if this material is as black as Pincus says it is".

Levi goes up to the nuns and grabs one of their sleeves. Comparing it to his own he mutters under his breath and walks off angrily.

One nun says to the other, "I didn't know Jews spoke Latin?"

"Me neither," said the other. "What did he say?"

"I think he said, "marcus pincus fuckedus."

580. ☆ ☆ ☆ ☆ ☆ ☆ ☆ ☆ ☆

It was a cold and sleet filled day in 1944 Brooklyn. Uncle Sol was pushing his vegetable cart up the street yelling "Hitler! Hitler!"

A policeman came running over and asked, "What's going on?"

"Nothing officer," Uncle Sol said. "When people come out to see what's going on, I sell them a banana."

"Does it work?" asked the cop.

"You tell me," said Uncle Sol. "Do you want a banana... or maybe a nice cumquat?"

"I know your tiger mom is a pain in the tushi, but I have to deal with a matza mom!"

581. ☆ ☆ ☆ ☆ ☆ ☆ ☆ ☆

A young man fell a sleep at the beach and got himself a terrible sunburn. At the emergency room the doctor gave him a tub of salve and a Viagra pill.

"What's the pill for?" asked the man. "With this sunburn, I'm not gonna have sex for a while."

"That's true," said the doctor. "The salve is for the sunburn and the Viagra will keep the sheet off you so you can sleep more comfortably tonight."

582. ☆ ☆ ☆ ☆ ☆ ☆ ☆ ☆

Sue and Sam wanted to join the Methodist church so they signed up to take a class on how to become good Methodists.

There were two other couples in the class, both much older than

Sue and Sam. The pastor who taught the class was a kindly older man who showed great patience throughout the course.

During the second-to-last class, the pastor told the couples that there was only one last task that they needed to do— abstain from sex for one week, so that they could have a symbolic first night of marriage as a proper Methodist couple.

The following week the minister asked each couple if they abstained from sex, the two older couples said yes, but Sue and Sam hung their heads in shame.

Sam tried to explain, "We tried really hard, but on the third morning, Sue dropped some cereal on the floor. As she bent over, I just lost control... I'm sorry it was all my fault. We gave into our animal lust right then on the floor."

"I'm sorry Samuel and Susan," the pastor said softly, "you are not welcome in the Methodist church."

"That makes sense," Susan said while bowing her head. "We're not welcome at the grocery store anymore either."

It is best to use the name of a major local grocery store in the punchline. It is a lot more personal that way. I once told this joke to the manager of my local Safeway store and she laughed heartily. She said, "We have that problem here sometimes, but it's always in cars at the back of the parking lot."

583.   ☆ ☆ ☆ ☆ ☆ ☆ ☆ ☆ ☆

An old disheveled man said to the bank teller, "I want to open a fucking checking account."

"Certainly sir," the kind lady said. "But, please watch your language this is a respectable banking establishment."

"I didn't come in here for a fuckin' civics lesson," the old man said. "I just want to open a fuckin' checking account."

The teller found herself flustered and politely excused herself, "Please allow me to get the manager to assist you, sir."

Within moments the teller returned with the manager, and the old man forced the check he wanted to deposit into the manager's hand, "I want to open a fuckin' account!"

The manager examined the check and calmly said, "I see you won the 10 million dollar lottery and this bitch is giving you trouble?"

584.   ☆ ☆ ☆ ☆ ☆ ☆ ☆

My mother believes that I am still as Catholic as she is. One day she found my diaphragm so I had to tell a lie, "Oh that, that's a swimming cap for my cat."

I sure hope my cat isn't going to hell for using a diaphragm.

"Noah! Don't let the elephants learn anything from those rabbits!"

585. ✩ ✩ ✩ ✩ ✩ ✩ ✩ ✩ ✩ ✩

According to George Carlin, "Anyone driving faster than you is an idiot, and anyone driving slower than you is a moron."

When it comes to telling jokes, you have to play to your audience. And for every audience that loves a joke you can find an audience that will want to lynch you for the same joke.

I grew up watching Johnny Carson. On a regular basis he would tell a joke about President Lincoln that would fail miserably. Then he would turn to Ed McMann and say, "Too soon?" Then he got his big laugh.

I once told a great joke to the wrong audience. When I was done I wanted to discontinue my talk and go find a hole to die in.

The situation occurred when I was talking to a church's men's club, but I thought I was talking to a Rotary Club. I tend to start my talks with a few jokes before getting down to the business at hand.

The joke I told was:

586. ☆ ☆ ☆ ☆ ☆ ☆ ☆ ☆ ☆

"Thanks to all you business men for taking time out from your busy day. You folks are some fancy dressers. I see some very nice ties in the audience... make sure you eat carefully or you will stain your ties that probably cost more than my car.

"I do not like wearing ties. I don't like where they point. Ties even come with a little arrow at the end, what's with that?" My mother taught me not to point."

At this point I lost my audience. Then I apologized profusely and restarted my talk. Luckily for me they were a forgiving group and my talk was accepted warmly.

I personally believe that you can joke about any subject. But, that doesn't mean that your audience will appreciate the joke. (Even if they tell it later to their friends.)

Jokes about death, Hitler, murder and such terrible subjects have their place. It is your job to know if you are in such a place when you tell highly offensive jokes.

I am told by my Uncle Sol that in the 1940's a common stage joke at the Jewish resorts in the Catskills was:

A comedian would walk onto the stage dressed as a German soldier and walk back and forth a little bit. Then something would catch his attention so he would take a second look. After a minute he would look surprised and snap to attention, clicking his heels and raising his right arm, "Heil..."

He would look uncomfortable and restart his salute. This time snapping crisply to attention, arm raised high, and shouting at the top of his lungs, "Heil...!"

Then the man on stage would relax and look sheepishly at the audience and ask, "What is that fellow's name again?"

The following cartoon proves that even horrible subjects can be funny.

"First the Holocaust, now this!"

4. Tall tales

587. ☆ ☆ ☆ ☆ ☆ ☆ ☆ ☆ ☆

My uncle was a leg puller from an early age. When he was in high school he lost the top of his index finger while building a chicken coop. Well, the truth be told, he didn't lose it. He knows exactly where it fell just before a chicken picked it up and swallowed it.

When he was in college he worked as a tour bus guide showing tourists around Hollywood. He showed celebrity homes and even went through the cemetery and told tales of how a few famous people died.

I think his favorite tall tales were told when a kid would ask him how he lost his finger.

"Well you see sonny," he would puff, "I wore it off pointing out all these attractions to you tourists."

"No really mister," the youngster would say, "How did you really lose it?"

"Well the truth be told, a few years ago this very bus was hijacked by some ruffians from the valley. I put my hand in my pocket and pretended I had a gun. A scuffle ensued and it accidentally went off."

He paused and shook his head as he glanced under the kid's seat. "And I never did find the tip of my finger."

588. ☆ ☆ ☆ ☆ ☆ ☆ ☆ ☆ ☆

At the police dog training club, Hal was getting lots of pats on the back because his dog had made the local paper. A gas station had been robbed at gun point.

"The car chase started just past midnight. The suspect was moving at a high rate of speed down 101. My team was called in after he was apprehended. The arresting officers found no weapon on the suspect or in the vehicle."

With a smile, Hal boasted to the small crowd. "As usual, they needed my dog's help to find the gun. Rex and I walked the median of that highway until 4 AM. I'd guess fifteen miles if it was an inch. But good old Rex found that gun. Again, Rex and I protected you folks and this fair city as you slumbered unaware of the real perils of this hardened city at night."

Uncle Willie wasn't one to let his dogs' exploits go untold.

"I'm sure Rex made you look good as you strolled the park like area between the highways. But my dog Buddy, he's a real hero. One night Buddy barked frantically and woke the whole house up. He ran from bedroom to bedroom making sure the family was alerted to the fire in the basement.

"As we gathered on the front lawn, we were fighting tears as we watched our home become engulfed in flames. The brave firefighters did their best, but the house was too far gone.

"Then I realized that Buddy was not with us. We were frantic. We all called for him. The fire chief told us that there was no way anyone could survive such a horrible blaze.

"Then through the smoke, Buddy stumbled down the front porch steps. He was smoldering and charred. He dropped from exhaustion and smoke inhalation at my feet.

"I knelt down and made sure he was alive. He was… just barely. In his mouth there was a wet paper towel wrapped around something. I unrolled it and found our fire insurance policy that we usually keep in the safe in the basement."

Hal laughed and patted Buddy on the head. "He sure looks good for a burned up dog."

"Well that's because we loved him back from the brink of death," Uncle Willie said.

Phil had listened to all this and added his two cents. "Well my Jazz was called in to help the police find an escaped convict. Hal, you must have been sleeping in after one of your long strolls in the park or something. The chief called and begged for my Jazz's help. He must have heard about how good a tracker my Jazz is.

"The escaped man was a murderer or rapist or something even nastier. Even though it was extremely inconvenient, I had to help. I met the police chief at the jail and asked for the guard to bring something that the escapee had been in close contact with.

"The guard returned lickity split with the convict's pillow. I lowered it to Jazz, and with just one sniff, she lifted her head high and inhaled the wind. Then she was off, dragging me as fast as I could run.

"Finally I had to release her from the leash. She was so focussed on getting this bad guy, she was unaware that she was ripping my arm from its socket.

"I hopped into the sheriff's Jeep and 16 vehicles followed her for 20 minutes. She went over the hills to the west of the jail. Forded the river and tunneled through the brambles. I could see she was bleeding, but she never slowed her pursuit.

"Over the next ridge we caught up with her as she barked furiously at the large doors to an old barn. The police and deputies surrounded the structure.

"Then Jazz started tearing at the decaying wood doors with her paws. She made just enough of an opening to squeeze through. The cops had no choice but to follow her in. Once inside, Jazz was growling intently at the far end of the barn. We crept up behind her and found a few hundred abandoned chicken coops. Jazz attacked one of the coop doors, ripping the mesh door clean off and sticking her head and shoulders in. She pulled out a matted clump of straw and feathers.

"I was so embarrassed. 'No Jazz,' I yelled, 'we don't care where the feathers in the pillow came from we want the man!'

Jazz dropped the matted straw and bolted out of the barn heading east…

589.   ☆ ☆ ☆ ☆ ☆ ☆ ☆ ☆ ☆

An old man was telling his grandchildren a story of how hard things were when he was a kid.

"When times were hard, we had to eat alligator for dinner. But it wasn't that bad. My mother was amazing in the kitchen. She could make a meal fit for a king, even out of alligator.

"You see, she had this foolproof recipe for cooking gator. This way she knew she was going to make a great meal.

"What she did was to take the gator and put it in a big pot of water, in another pot, she place a large rock, about the same size as the alligator.

"Then she would pour in a bunch of water and salt and boil both pots on the stove. She knew that when she could poke into that rock with a fork, that there alligator was about half cooked."

590. ☆ ☆ ☆ ☆ ☆ ☆ ☆ ☆ ☆ ☆

Sherlock Holmes and Dr. John Watson were on a train. As they passed a large herd of cows, Homes announce, "318."

"318? What on Earth are you talking about?" asked Watson.

"Cows my good man, cows."

"How on Earth did you count the cows so quickly?" asked Watson.

"Good heavens," Homes chortled. "No one could do that with just a glimpse. I used deductive reasoning. I simply counted the legs and divided by four."

591. ☆ ☆ ☆ ☆ ☆ ☆ ☆ ☆ ☆ ☆

I once met the Queen of England in an airpot. To my surprise I got really nervous. I didn't know what to do. Should I bow, shake her Royal hand, or curtsey?

I had only ever seen her on a stamp, so I nonchalantly walked behind her and licked the back of her head.

The Royal Secret Service was not impressed with my actions and I was detained for a few hours. It all worked out in the end.

The Queen called for a few weeks, but once she understood that I was married, she stopped. I didn't have to get a restraining order or anything like that.

592. ☆ ☆ ☆ ☆ ☆ ☆ ☆ ☆ ☆ ☆

A city slicker gets a flat tire in front of a farmhouse. The farmer comes out to see if he can be of any assistance.

"You wouldn't happen to have a jack I could use? Mine busted and I need to put on my spare," the city slicker said.

"Be happy to help, why don't I have my pig do that for ya, it's supper time and I'm sure Ma would want me to invite ya in," the farmer said.

"Your pig?" the city slicker asked thinking he misunderstood.

"Yeah. I got me one handy pig. He can swap out a tire for you in no time, let's go wash up for dinner." With that the farmer whistled and a three legged pig came running out of the barn behind the farmhouse.

The closer he got the stranger he looked.

The three legged pig was missing an eye, an ear, and also had some nasty scars along one side.

The farmer told the pig the problem and the pig commenced to fetching the car jack and switching out the tire.

On the way to the farmhouse, the city fella asked, "That's some amazing pig you got!"

"You don't know the half of it," the farmer said. "Last Christmas Eve, that there pig saved my whole family when the house caught fire. He broke out of his sty, woke me and ma, and as we were figuring out what was going on he pulled our boy out of the house, saving his life."

"Is that how he lost his leg?" the city man asked.

"Nope. He got out safe too." The farmer said. "Then that damn fool went inside the house again, pulled out the burning Christmas tree, keeping the fire from spreading. He saved most of our home. Sorry to say, that's how he got so scared and lost his ear and his eye."

"How'd he loose his leg?"

"Well, a pig that valuable you don't eat all at once, do ya!"

"Statistically, one in seven dwarfs are grumpy."

593. ☆ ☆ ☆ ☆ ☆ ☆ ☆ ☆ ☆

An aging hippie showed up at a small country church asking for work in exchange for food. The reverend offered him three hots and a cot for up to a week in exchange for painting the small building.

The down on his luck hippie happily agreed.

The minister gave him $100 to go and buy 5 gallons of paint from the country store across the way. Somehow our hippie painter was able to get lost crossing the street and ended up behind the high school buying pot. After a little relaxing smoke, the hippie painter went to the store to buy the paint. He only had enough for 3 gallons of paint so he decided to make it go further with paint thinner, figuring no one would ever know.

Just as he was finishing the paint job, the skies got nasty and a terrible rainstorm washed the new paint job off the church. The old hippie was beside himself with grief as he fell to his knees and prayed, "Oh God, what should I do?"

A booming voice echoed from the heavens and God said, "Repaint, repaint and thin no more!"

594. ☆ ☆ ☆ ☆ ☆ ☆ ☆ ☆

Cyril wanted desperately to impress this girl so he booked reservations at the Top of the Plaza. While his date was in the powderroom there was a lot of excitement and Robin Williams and entourage entered the restaurant. Thinking on his feet, Cyril decide to ask Mr. Williams for a little help. He sheepishly approached Mr. Williams' table and hand-gestured if he could talk. Mr. Williams graciously waved him forward.

"Sorry to bother you, my name is Cyril. I'm trying to impress my date. Would you be so kind as to come by our table and act like you know me?"

Mr. Williams thought for a moment and took a small pad of paper from his coat pocket. As he wrote he said, "When I come over, you say this to me." Then he handed Cyril the note.

Cyril memorize the note and hid it in his pocket.

At the end of the evening, Robin Williams came over with great fan fair, to Cyril's table. "Cyril, is that you. How nice to see you... did you get that script I sent you? I so hope you can work on that project with me... You have to get on board. I'd be lost without your input!"

Cyril was nervously stunned but recited his lines perfectly. "Robin, I'm on a date! You know I don't like mixing business with pleasure, so please don't take this the wrong way, but fuck off!"

595. ☆ ☆ ☆ ☆ ☆ ☆ ☆ ☆ ☆

Bubba won the lottery and decided to build the biggest house in the sleepy town of Red Bluff. He spared no expense to get the house of his dreams. He even went to Redding to get a highly praised architect.

Bubba showed the blueprints to the best contractor in Red Bluff who shook his head with concern.

"Bubba, you don't want me to build you this house do ya?"

"Yeah I do," said Bubba. "Exactly as the architect drew it."

"But Bubba," the builder said, "there's a huge mistake in these here plans."

"I want that exact house!" stomped Bubba.

"OK!" said the builder under his breath as he walked away. "You'll be surprised when you find you have two bathrooms!"

596. ☆ ☆ ☆ ☆ ☆ ☆ ☆ ☆ ☆

I got married by a judge. I should've asked for a jury.

597. ☆ ☆ ☆ ☆ ☆ ☆ ☆ ☆ ☆

Have you ever heard a pterodactyl pee?
You never will either, the 'p' in pterodactyl is silent.

598. ☆ ☆ ☆ ☆ ☆ ☆ ☆ ☆ ☆

A man got into the pleasant routine of eating his lunch at the zoo. He would relax on a park bench across the path from the gorilla cage and watch the primates watch him. After a few months, he seemed to be building a rapport with the largest male gorilla. The man often, when no one was watching, threw part of his sandwich into the cage. The large gorilla seemed to appreciate the human's generosity. Over many more months, the man noticed that the large male gorilla was mimicking his posture.

To test his theory he patted himself on the head. Then the gorilla patted himself on his head. The man flapped his arms, and so did the gorilla.

Accidentally during the test, the man got too close to the cage and the gorilla suddenly reached out and grabbed him. Within seconds the gorilla pummeled the poor man almost to death.

During the long recovery in the hospital, the man schemed on a way to get back at the gorilla. He built his plan in his mind and the day he was released from the hospital, the man went to the zoo to seek his revenge.

He took his bag of goodies to the cage and found the gorilla sitting calmly.

Standing far back, the man patted his head hoping the gorilla would copy him. The gorilla did. Then the man flapped his arms. The gorilla copied him. Then the man took out two knives and a large salami from his bag. He threw one of the knives to the feet of the gorilla.

The man placed the large salami up between his legs and waved it around. The gorilla seemed curious and he took his giant gorillahood and waved it around. The man took the knife and in one vicious slice he cut the salami in half.

The gorilla stood up tall and with one finger he gently pulled down his lower eye lid.

The man was furious, again he went through the cutting off the salami routine, and again the gorilla gently took one finger and pulled down his lower eye lid.

Just then the gorilla keeper walked by, "Hey mister you may want to know, that thing he's doing with his eyelid, that means 'fuck you' in gorilla."

599.   ☆ ☆ ☆ ☆ ☆ ☆ ☆ ☆

Enthusiastic Hillary Clinton supporters really wanted her to run for president. The group made bumper stickers that read, "Run Hillary Run".

The bumper stickers sold amazingly well because, Democrats put them on their back bumpers, and Republicans put them on their front bumpers.

600.   ☆ ☆ ☆ ☆ ☆ ☆ ☆ ☆

Morty died and went to heaven. On his first day he is shown

around by an angel. Morty is amazed at how beautiful and peaceful heaven is. It is just as he always imagined it would be.

When they end up at the heavenly cafeteria, Morty is almost in tears with joy when he finds out that all the food in heaven has no calories. "You can eat whatever you wish," the angel says. "No guilt or worry, you're in heaven."

All of a sudden, there is a commotion. A tall man dressed in hospital scrubs barges into the line and pushes people out of his way as he grabs food and mutters under his breath.

"What's this all about?" Morty asks the angel.

"Oh, that's just God. Sometimes he thinks he's a doctor."

601.   ☆ ☆ ☆ ☆ ☆ ☆ ☆ ☆ ☆ ☆

Scientists learned that men pass gas more often than women do. After much research and millions of dollars it was shown to be due to the fact that woman never shut up long enough to build up pressure.

602. ☆ ☆ ☆ ☆ ☆ ☆ ☆ ☆ ☆

Pete and Rosemarie have been married for over fifty years. One morning Rosemarie was feeling a little romantic and suggested that they eat breakfast in the buff, "Like the old days when we were young and adventurous."

So Pete and Rosemarie enjoyed breakfast in the sun room. During breakfast they were happily reminiscing.

After about twenty minutes, Rosemarie said, "I'm starting to feel a little tingle of excitement."

"But Rosemarie, it isn't Saturday night, what are you talking about?"

"You know honey, remember when you were reckless and couldn't get enough? I remember how you ravaged me many a time in this very room. In fact, just thinking about it is making my nipples hot…"

"Oh Rosemarie," Peter interrupted, "your boobs are in your oatmeal."

603. ☆ ☆ ☆ ☆ ☆ ☆ ☆ ☆ ☆

After eating at a Japanese restaurant, Murray notices that his farts are weird. Instead of just bbbbppptttt they now go bbbbppptttt-honda.

Over the next two weeks Murray realizes that whenever he eats he goes bbbbppptttt-honda.

Concerned, he goes to the doctor who can't figure out what is going on, so he is sent to a specialist. Still no answer.

Getting a little worried, Murray decides to go to a Japanese doctor thinking that maybe it was something he caught at the Japanese restaurant.

Murray tells Dr. Fuji the problem, and Dr. Fuji tells him that he can cure it.

Dr. Fuji takes a huge needle and puts it into Murray's side and draws out some nasty gook. Lots and lots of nasty gook.

"American doctors don't know," Dr. Fuji explains, "but all Japanese doctors know…. Abscess makes the fart go honda."

604.   ☆ ☆ ☆ ☆ ☆ ☆ ☆ ☆ ☆

A traffic cop was sitting on the corner of a city street when a flash went by and his radar gun read 76 MPH. Not sure what he just saw, he took off after it. He clocked speeds over 110 miles per hour when he saw that he was chasing a 3 legged chicken.

The 3 legged chicken took a sharp left and went down an alley. When the cop got to the end of the ally he found an old warehouse with a sign that read, *Poultry Research Institute*.

The cop went inside where he found a gaggle of scientists looking at regular old chickens in cages and talking.

He told them what he had seen and they explained that their research goal was to grow a chicken with three legs because market research showed that most families want the extra leg so the kids won't squabble at the dinner table.

"Interesting," said the cop. "How's it taste?"

The researchers looked embarrassed till one said, "Don't know, haven't been able to catch it."

5. True stories

It is often stated, "truth is stranger than fiction." This section proves that saying to be true. Most of these stories happened to me and my family. The rest happened to patients, friends or colleagues. I'll tell you which are which, but when it comes to patients, friends and colleagues I have changed the names to protect their ids, egos, and in some cases super egos.

605.   ☆ ☆ ☆ ☆ ☆ ☆ ☆ ☆ ☆

Hippie therapist

I wear my hair long. For one of my more conservative colleagues my hair was professionally inappropriate. Over a course of a few months, whenever I ran into Dr. Walters he quickly brought up my hair. He would ask questions like, "Don't you get concerned that people won't see you as professional?" "Are you unaware that in this community we therapists have a more conservative appearance?" "I haven't seen you at church, where do you attend?"

After months of this, he wanted to make sure that I knew he was not happy with my hair length. "I would be very happy to refer to you, but I can't if you continue to present yourself as a hippie."

I thanked him and moved on.

The next time I saw him he was outwardly upset with me, "How is your practice going... are you even able to afford a hair cut?"

"My practice is doing well," I said. "Thanks for asking. But when it comes to my hair, I choose to wear it like your lord and savior."

He was not amused with me and walked off briskly muttering, "blasphemy... blasphemy!" kind of under his breath.

A few weeks later, I was coming into a professional lunch gathering at a local restaurant and Dr. Walters met me at the conference room door.

"I'll make you a deal," he said very kindly as he held up a crisp 20 dollar bill. "I'll pay for your next hair cut."

I took the twenty. "Thanks, I was wondering how I was going to pay for lunch."

I left a $20 tip for my $8 lunch.

Dr. Walters and I don't talk much past, "Good morning," but he has been kind enough to refer clients to me regularly over the last 10 years.

"Let me get this straight... you want me to permanently disable this doorbell"

606. ☆☆☆☆☆☆☆☆☆☆

Satan and the chickens

When I was in graduate school I rented a room in a large older house. The house was surrounded by apricot orchards except one side was a neighboring house. The old man who lived next door kept to himself. Up to this point we never really talked, we would politely wave and smile at each other.

The old man raised chickens that he kept penned on the far side of his backyard. Most of the chickens were ordinary, but some were spectacular looking.

One day I came home and to my surprise found my German shepherd, Satan, lying happily by the chain linked fence that separated the two yards. On the old man's side of the fence were twelve of his spectacular chickens, headless. It was easy to surmise what had happened. The chickens had gotten out of their enclosure and as they poked their heads through the fence, Satan beheaded them. All twelve of them.

As I was standing there the old man came over. He was very understanding. He explained that as long as I punished the dog, he would not charge me for his prize chickens. I asked him how I should punish Satan.

He explained that the best way was to tie one of the dead chickens around the dog's neck for the rest of the day so he would learn that he didn't like chickens anymore. I was dubious that this would work, but I really wanted to solve this problem with my neighbor. (I definitely didn't have a way to pay for twelve prize chickens.) I also figured that it wouldn't hurt Satan.

So, I tied a carcass around Satan's neck. The old man was very happy and went back inside his house.

Satan seemed to like the idea of the chicken around his neck. He pranced around showing it off. He later took a nap using it as a pillow.

Around midnight, I cut the chicken off Satan and he appeared quite upset. It seemed like he had bonded with the carcass and wanted to keep his trophy of a hunt well done.

At 5 AM Satan was by my bed moaning and crying. He wanted to go out right away! I opened the back door and he ran out crouching. As soon as his paws hit the grass he started to poop. He was very uncomfortable as he crouched walked around the yard pooping out twelve beaks, one at a time, over a 5 minute period.

He definitely learned not to eat chicken heads.

607.   ☆☆☆☆☆☆☆☆

The drunk at 7-11

On a regular basis when someone asks me in public "How ya doing?" I answer, "I'm getting old." This tends to lead to a smile and even conversation. I think I have been saying this since I was 15 years old.

Often people will say, "You're not that old." In my thirties I found myself answering "It's not the years it's the milage." Most people over 40 would agree with a smile and a knowing nod.

The best response to "I'm getting old" came from an old homeless and intoxicated guy behind me in line at 7-11.

"How you doing?" asked the clerk.

"I'm getting old," I answered.

In a singsongy voice the old man said, as he lifted his wine bottle, "You're only as old as the woman you feel."

608.   ☆☆☆☆☆☆☆☆

Uncle Joe's Eye

What I remember best about Uncle Joe's house was going there after school and doing homework. Then mom would show up and say, "Let's go, the news is coming on. Uncle Joe doesn't like any noise during the news."

Most people in my family didn't seem to like Uncle Joe. But for me… I thought he was interesting. He told good stories and he was good at helping me with my homework. From what I could tell, he was really smart and he liked me. I knew that he did because he told me about how he lost his eye in the war and how he hated his glass eye because it hurt as the day wore on.

When I was ten years old my little brother Garry and I had to stay overnight at Uncle Joe's house. I only remember staying over night at Uncle Joe's house this one time.

When it was bedtime, Uncle Joe sent us kids up to bed. To our surprise, he didn't come and check on us or remind us to brush. He just sent us to bed. So we got ready and went to bed in his kid's old room. After a few minutes of laying in bed, Garry, the trouble maker, started to talk and one thing led to another.

Uncle Joe yelled upstairs, "What's the matter with you damn kids. I said go to bed damn-it! Don't make me come up there!"

For a few minutes we lay in the beds stiff as boards. We didn't hear swear words in our home, mom wouldn't allow it.

"Uncle Joe swore," Garry said.

"Yeah he said damn!" I added.

Garry busted a gut laughing.

"Shush Garry, he'll hear you," I whispered.

"Damn straight..." Garry said in a deep voice and we both started laughing uncontrollably.

The door opened with a slam and the room shook.

"What the hell is wrong with you kids, I said go to bed!" Uncle Joe roared. He was a big man and he blocked most of the light from the hallway.

"Phil started it..." Garry said.

"I don't care, who started it. I just want quiet!"

Uncle Joe left the doorway abruptly and returned in a second with a glass of water. He stood in the doorway and said calmly, "I'll find out the truth about which one of you boys is making all the noise!"

Then he reached up to his eye. He placed his finger in the eye socket and slowly popped out his glass eye. You could hear the slimy sound. He placed his eye into the glass of water and put the glass on the dresser. His eye bounced slightly then settled to the bottom. It was looking right at me. Staring right at me.

"Any more noise and I will know who is getting the belt!"

He slowly closed the door leaving a sliver of light on the glistening eye.

I lay in bed too scared to fully breath. I was pretty sure that he couldn't see out of that thing... but it seemed foolish to take any chances. I watched the shiny eye in complete silence for a very long time.

Years later I was in college reading an entry level psychology textbook. There, right on the page, they were talking about my Uncle Joe. I called my mom and told her, "Uncle Joe is an alcoholic!"

"That's not a nice way to talk about family," she said.

"But mom it's true he is textbook."

"I know, I know," she said. "Why do you think I never took you around Uncle Joe's or Aunt Rosa's house in the evening?"

"I thought it was because he liked to listen to Walter Cronkite in quiet?"

"Well, who doesn't love Walter Cronkite, but it really was that he was a stinking drunk!"

I didn't bring up the incident with Uncle Joe's eye.

609. ☆ ☆ ☆ ☆ ☆ ☆ ☆ ☆ ☆

My mom had one joke

My mother was not a very funny lady. She only had one joke and it was't much of a joke. However, I retell it here out of respect for a woman who put up with a lot of my antics over the years.

My mother was born on the fourth of July. So every year we heard:

"Isn't it nice that everyone takes July fourth off to celebrate my birthday?"

Even though Mrs. Copitch couldn't tell a joke she was funny… here are a few examples:

610. ☆ ☆ ☆ ☆ ☆ ☆ ☆ ☆ ☆

My mom and the two liter bottle of coke

I was a young teenager when 2 liter bottles first made their appearance in the stores. People thought they were too big. I thought they were great. One day I got a lecture from my mother about how drinking directly out of a 2 liter bottle was crude and unsanitary behavior as well as unsightly. Another example of the downfall of western civilization.

A few days later, while I was doing my homework, my mom asked if I wanted something to drink. She came in with a full 2-liter bottle with a baby bottle nipple securely attached to the top.

She placed it on the table without saying anything.

I heard howls of laughter coming from the kitchen as Aunt Hilda and my mom busted up.

I cut the tip of the nipple off, making the hole much larger, and sucked it all down over the course of the evening.

My mother never said a word.

Nowadays, bottle manufacturers sell bottles with fancy nipples. My mom was ahead of her time.

611.   ☆ ☆ ☆ ☆ ☆ ☆ ☆ ☆

My mom and the ambulance driver

My mother was tough and opinionated. Once she set her mind to something, it would take an act of congress to get her to reconsider. One afternoon I got a phone call from Mr. Braverman, the manager of the senior citizen apartments that my mom lived in. The apartments were a nice living situation. Everyone had their own small apartment, but the staff watched over everyone without being too obvious.

Well, Mr. Braverman called and told me that there was a problem, "Your mother took a fall and hurt her hip. She needs to go to the hospital."

"Did you call an ambulance?"

"Yes Dr. Copitch, we've called an ambulance, but your mother is refusing to go with them. I was hoping you could talk to her."

"Sure, put her on."

"Philip is that you?" mom said.

"Yes mom, what's going on?"

"Do you remember, Sadie Goldstein? You used to play with her boys back in the old neighborhood."

"No, what's going on, why won't you go to the hospital and get your hip looked at."

"I'm trying to tell you. Sadie Goldstein. You remember. Chubby lady. Used to dye her hair auburn, as if no one knew her color was out of a bottle."

"Mom, I don't remember the lady…"

"Well she had three boys. You remember, she was always saying that her oldest was as smart as you. You remember little Stevie? Asthmatic, slight boy, always a little uncoordinated."

I had no idea who she was talking about but I decided to play along with the conversation hoping to figure out what was going on. "Yeah, I think I remember, why?"

"Well, little Stevie is all grown up. He's the ambulance driver."

"Oh good," I said. "I remember. He was a really careful driver. He was a good boy mom, why won't you let him drive you to the hospital?"

"I'm telling you, why don't you ever listen to me. His mom, Sadie Goldstein, you remember her from the old neighborhood? She always said that her Stevie was going to be a doctor. But he's an ambulance driver."

"I'm sure he's a great ambulance driver, why won't you let him take you to the hospital?

"Philip, you want me to get into an ambulance with an <u>underachiever</u>?"

"Mom, put little Stevie Goldstein on, I want to talk to him."

"Sure, honey," she said.

"Hello?" Steven said.

"Hi, please let me help you get my mom to the hospital."

"Sure."

"OK, you're working your way through medical school as an ambulance driver. Understand?"

"Great. Got it. And I do remember you from PS-35. Next time you're in town we should get together," Steven said.

"Thanks Steve, sorry about the hassle."

612.   ☆ ☆ ☆ ☆ ☆ ☆ ☆ ☆

When Garry and I visited mom after being away for a long time.

It turned out that Garry and I were going to be in New York at the same time. So we decided to go visit our mom in Rochester for one day. At the time it seemed easier than having to explain how we were in New York City and didn't make the one hour flight to visit.

Mom was so excited that we were visiting and offered to make our favorite dishes for dinner.

When we got to mom's tiny apartment the table was set with all of our favorite foods. Bagels and lox, whitefish, roast beef, mashed potatoes and gravy, and an assortment of candies and noshes.

We were going to be in town for 26 hours, there was no way we could eat it all, but we did try. My mother was a very good cook. Not a health conscious cook, but a good cook. She would start with butter then add some potatoes. Not that I'm complaining mind you, but I know where this story is going.

Garry and I sat down and got to use the good china. This was a big deal. My mother still has the same couch and chairs from when we were kids. We were never allowed to sit on them. They were for the plastic to sit on, and the plastic only came off if someone died or the rabbi visited. The good china was reserved for the rabbi or weddings.

There were only two place settings at the table.

"Who has time to sit? My boys are home, I have things to do," my mother said.

Throughout the meals, yes I did say meals, my mother would come out of the kitchen holding a large pot, "Do you want some more potatoes, they're your favorite. I made them just the way you like them, with love."

"I'm stuffed mom," I said.

"So you only need a dollop," she said as she splatted a mound of potatoes on my plate. Looking at Garry, "You want some more? I'll only have to throw them away, God forbid."

"NO thanks mom, I'm..."

Splat! The potatoes hit Garry's plate.

My mother never believed in serving spoons. She liked the large army style cooking utensils. "Only one spoonful, you've got to keep up your strength."

Garry leaned over to me and said, "I have to go for a smoke, don't tell mom. I told her I stopped smoking years ago."

"Mom, it was great, I have to go for a walk, great food," he said as he walked out of the apartment.

Mom walked out of the kitchen holding her giant pot, "I know he is smoking, you should talk to him about that filthy habit. You would think I have enough cancer in me for the whole family!"

"Mom, he is a good..."

"I know, I know. I worry about him, he's my baby... you want some more potatoes." Holding up a platoon size serving on a large metal spoon.

"No thanks, I've had enough," I said pointing to the mound of potatoes still on my plate.

"What, you don't like my cooking?" she said sadly.

"Mom you're a great cook. I'm stuffed."

Mom looked around the room making sure we were alone. "Philip, you know me, I don't like to complain, but it looks like you've put on a few pounds."

613. ☆ ☆ ☆ ☆ ☆ ☆ ☆ ☆

Sleeping on the hide-a-bed

The night after the big feast mom wanted us to set up the hide-a-bed. It was a twin size bed with strategically placed metal cross beams intended to castrate any man that moved in his sleep.

On the flight to mom's house I called the floor and Garry agreed to the hide-a-bed. I should have know something was up when he agreed to sleep in the Marquis de Sade torture bed so easily.

At bedtime Garry said, "Mom, Phil doesn't want you to know but his back has been giving him trouble. So I offered to sleep on the floor, but he just yelled at me."

"Philip, you should sleep on the bed. Your father had a bad back, it is best if you take care of yourself," Mom explained.

I ended up on the hide-a-bed. The bar of dismemberment gouged into my hip, and the springs sang my movements.

After Garry and I were settled in for a few minutes, mom came back with a glass of ginger ale and a doily, "In case your back is too painful here is some ginger ale and two aspirin."

"Can I have some ginger ale?" Garry asked from the floor.

"Of course not, you're not ill." Mom said.

Then mom started to pick up my socks off the floor.

"I'm going to be doing some delicates in the sink, I thought I would wash your socks for you."

A few minutes later, mom was in the bathroom talking to herself, "God forbid my boys should pick up after themselves. For years now I would say, 'take care of your belongings,' but no, they don't listen."

After Garry and I were asleep, mom came into the living-room to open the window. When she stepped on Garry we were instantly awake. To see what was going on, I turned over on the bar of shame, raking my boy parts. I groaned with discomfort.

"Are you OK Philip?" mom asked as she tried to walk around Garry in the dark.

"I'm OK," I lied. "It's just, ah... my back."

"Do you want me to massage it for you?"

"NO! No thanks mom," I said.

Garry figured out what was what, "Phil you should let mom massage your pains, she was a nurse you know."

We both laughed.

Mom was at the living-room window with a ruler—measuring.

"What are you doing mom?" I asked."

I want your window opened three inches.

As Garry and I attempted to go back to sleep, mom was in her room closing her window and muttering to herself. "God forbid I use the air my boys need."

614. ☆ ☆ ☆ ☆ ☆ ☆ ☆ ☆ ☆

Mom and the new TV

Later on in years my mother was riddled with cancer. She was a tough woman that just seemed to muddle through. One year I decided to buy her a large color console television with this new added feature—a remote control. I figured that it would be easier for her not to have to get out of bed on the "bad" days.

When I went to visit her, her old black and white TV was sitting on top of the new color console.

"Mom is the new TV working OK, any problem? It has a warrantee," I said.

"It works just fine but the screen is so big. You know what they say about the new color TV's."

"Is something wrong with the picture?"

"The picture is wonderful, it's just so big and it's in color."

"What's wrong with color, mom?" I asked.

"You know, it gives you cancer."

"What, that's not right, color TV's don't give you cancer."

"I heard that they do," she said.

"Mom you already have cancer, you have nothing to worry

about. Where's the remote control?"

"I put it in the sideboard in the living-room. I don't want it in this room."

"But mom, I got it especially to make things easier for you. You can change the channels from your bed." I explained.

"But Philip, my eyes aren't what they used to be, what if I miss the TV and hit the chair or the curtains. I don't want to burn the place down."

"Mom, it's not a laser beam it's a channel changer," I said.

"I know that, I'm not daft, but it is red. It said so on the box," Mom pointed out.

"Infrared mom. It won't cause a fire."

I don't know how it happened, but the new TV ended up at my sister's house and mom happily enjoyed her old black and white. Somehow I ended up buying my older sister a color console television for her living-room.

615.   ☆ ☆ ☆ ☆ ☆ ☆ ☆ ☆ ☆

Geri Copitch and the San Francisco Airport

My wife is always late. Early in our relationship she was often very late. She has gotten much better with her tardiness over the years.

Many years ago, Geri was getting ready to fly from San Francisco to New York. I found myself prodding her along the night before to finish packing so she could get some sleep.

In the morning I checked with the airline concerning flight times. I was informed that the flight was delayed at least one hour and forty-five minutes due to fog.

I decided to see what would happen, so I didn't tell Geri about the schedule change. "I'm ready to go when you are," I said, and I sat on the couch without another word.

When we finally got in the car, we were behind time. Driving up the highway to the airport we hit traffic. We were further behind time. I said nothing. Geri got more and more worried about missing her flight.

At the airport parking lot she was so upset, I just had to tell her that all was fine and the fight was delayed.

Luckily for me she didn't divorce me that very day.

"I had them neutered and declawed, now they're basically pillows that eat."

616. ☆ ☆ ☆ ☆ ☆ ☆ ☆ ☆ ☆

Michael and the teacher's dress

I went to Public School-35 when I was a kid. My best friend was Michael. Michael was a great friend who often took the full blame for stuff we both did.

Our 5th grade teacher was Mrs. Manchester. The prettiest teacher in the whole wide world. She also smelled really good. There was a rumor going around school that Mrs. Manchester didn't wear any underwear. Michael and I were fascinated by this tidbit of information. So I developed a plan, I would drop a pencil when Mrs. Manchester was helping me at my desk. As she picked it up, Michael would take a quick peek up her dress.

The caper was afoot. Mrs. Manchester came to help me. She put her hands on her knees and slouched down the way she did. I dropped my pencil. She bent forward and Michael peeked. A stupid girl laughed and Mrs. Manchester straighten up abruptly catching Michael's head under the back of her dress. He fell flat on his face between her feet.

Michael had a nice talk with the principal. Mrs. Voss was an angry lady who we were all fearful of. She had one arm that just hung there like it had no bones. She often would hold her own hand by swinging the dead arm up and catching it. She was a very scary principal.

Michael didn't tell Mrs. Voss about me. Which was good 'cause my mother would have killed me. Michael's dad just beat him. He was fine in a few days.

I suppose you want to know. Mrs. Manchester wore black panties.

617. ☆ ☆ ☆ ☆ ☆ ☆ ☆ ☆

Michael skeeching down Monroe Avenue

My best friend Michael had no fear. Unlike me, he didn't seem to care if he got dead. On winter days lots of the boys would skeech to school. Skeeching is when you crouch behind a car holding onto the bumper. You could slide down slush covered Monroe Avenue, skiing on your boots all the way to school in no time.

Drivers were not happy with skeechers, and the young cops would try to nab you. The old cops were too fat to run so they would pretend not to see you. You had to grab the bumper at a light without being seen by the driver.

There were a few dangerous things about skeeching. The roads were slippery, so if you lost hold, you had to stay out of the way of the next car. That usually wasn't a problem, because the next car could see you, so they gave you a little more room. Some of the old Italian men would swear at you, but most just laughed at you 'cause they did the same thing when they were kids.

You did want to stay away from the tailpipe. If you weren't careful, your brain would be confused until second period from "sucking tailpipe" all the way down Monroe Avenue.

But by far the biggest problem were dry patches in the road

slush. At 35 miles per hour, if your boots hit a dry patch, it would lay you out and you would be dragged down the street on your belly.

One block from school was a furniture warehouse. The boxy furniture trucks were the best ride. They didn't have back doors just a canvas back drape covered by a thick metal mesh fence. If you grabbed the mesh you could put your belly on the truck's oversized bumper and ride to school with your legs dangling off the back.

One snowy morning, Michael and I caught a ride on a furniture truck. I was holding on with both hands as the truck raced down the road. Michael yelled that he was slipping. It was hard to hear over the wind, the rattling truck body, and the old diesel engine. His one handed grip was failing. Then at the intersection of Meg and Monroe, the truck hit a pothole. Mike was launched off the back of the truck and landed faced down at 35 miles an hour. Cars screeched and horns blared. I was sure Michael was dead. At the next light, I jumped off the truck and ran back a block. Mike was standing in the intersection, cars stopped all around him. Michael had his pants down to his knees and he was holding his crotch, hopping up and down and yelling, "I broke my dick, I broke my dick."

Over the next two weeks, Michael showed everyone who asked. He went from a swollen bright red to deep blue the first day. Then to blue and yellow, then to mostly yellow. We never told any adults, especially his dad.

About a month later, on the way to school Michael just threw out, "It doesn't hurt to pee any more."

618. ☆ ☆ ☆ ☆ ☆ ☆ ☆ ☆

Garry and the summer of holy cow

When my little brother was 13 he would get stuck on a phrase and say it so often it would drive you crazy. One month he said "holy cow" constantly. Once on a long boring car ride to go camping in the Adirondack Mountains, Garry said, "holy cow" so many times that he was threatened with death. A huge family fight broke out and ended up in painful silence. Anger filled every part of the station wagon. The tension was unbearable.

After about ten minutes, someone gently pointed out that there was a huge field of black cows, thousands of them—and one white cow.

Thirty seconds later Garry softly said, "Holy cow."
You had to be there... that was funny!

619. ☆ ☆ ☆ ☆ ☆ ☆ ☆ ☆ ☆

Expensive chocolate

My wife Geri, came home burdened with grocery bags. A few minutes went by and she delicately handed me a little piece of foil wrapped chocolate.

"Enjoy your $1,635 piece of chocolate," she said softly.

"What?" I said.

"I got it for you from the accountant when I picked up and payed the accounting bill for our taxes."

620. ☆ ☆ ☆ ☆ ☆ ☆ ☆ ☆ ☆ ☆

Jazz and the obstacle course

In my younger days my hobby was training police dogs. I had this one dog Jazz, that made me look like I knew what I was doing.

Part of the training was getting the dog to be comfortable following commands no matter what the environment. So, I taught Jazz to jump up onto tables, shimmy under low structures, and jump through windows. All this was done with small hand commands. This was trust practice, because Jazz didn't know what was on the other side until she got there.

One day I was walking behind an apartment building having Jazz practice around real life items, such as abandoned old cars and large city dumpsters.

We came upon a large dumpster and from 20 feet away I waved the command for Jazz to jump onto it. Jazz leaped and all of a sudden she was gone. Then her front paws and head popped out. She happily awaited my next command. The dumpster top was open and I accidentally had her jump into it. I felt terrible. I'm sure glad no one will ever know.

621.   ☆ ☆ ☆ ☆ ☆ ☆ ☆ ☆

Jazz goes to second grade

When I worked for a child abuse treatment agency, I was often invited to talk to school children about scary issues. Jazz often accompanied me and would always steal the show.

Jazz was well versed in subtle hand signals and would easily perform complex tasks without the kids knowing we were working together.

One part of our "act" was to talk about safety, explains that sometimes adults will tell kids what to do for their own safety. During this part of the talk, behind my back, Jazz would jump up on the teacher's desk and earn a time out for sitting on the furniture! When she got her time out, Jazz would ham it up by slinking and pouting her way to the designated time out area where she had to sit quietly and think about her misbehavior. The kids loved it and would howl with laughter when she got her consequence. After her time out was done, I talked to Jazz about her responsibilities and the importance of caring and sharing. The kids were transfixed and would nod in agreement.

Often, after Jazz and I visited, the teacher would have the kids write us thank you notes. The notes and drawings were precious.

One boy wrote:

    Dear Jazz and Dr. Phil,

Thanks for visiting my class. I love Jazz. My dog had a big fat tick. It popped this morning.

Love, Joey

622.   ☆ ☆ ☆ ☆ ☆ ☆ ☆ ☆ ☆

You're not fat, Dr. Phil...

I like self deprecating humor. When I make myself the victim of the punchline I can often relax a group. The shrink in me thinks it is interesting that often members of the audience will try to protect me from my own facts. For example, if I am talking to a group of parents about helping children learn self control I will often say, "It's hard to have self control. Even for us adults. I don't know if you have noticed, but I'm fat. It's my choice because I eat too much, but it is important to remember how hard self control is to accomplish when helping our children to grow up."

It is not unusual for some kind soul to say, "You're not fat, Dr. Phil. You're big boned."

"I don't know about my bones, but I'm fat because I eat too much."

"No Dr. Phil," another person offers. "Maybe you have a thyroid problem."

I point this out because it is funny that some people would rather I have a thyroid problem than an eat-too-much-by-choice problem.

By using self deprecating humor you can often open a discussion about hard subjects.

"Nice shirt Dr. Phil."

"Thanks," I smile, "I do all my shopping at Omar the tent makers."

Recently at the martial arts dojo a little 10 year old fellow was baiting his mother and inadvertently questioning my authority to manage the class.

I looked sternly down at the tiny student and said in my sensei[14] voice, "You do know I have heartburn that's bigger than you."

The mom laughed and the child lost his control over her. So he had no choice but to return to his class.

A friend's child asked me why I have such big dogs.

"Ya know Tommy," I said as I patted my belly. "I haven't seen my feet since 1942. So I don't want any dog running around me that I could accidentally step on."

Another example of self deprecating humor that often is helpful in my work:

---

[14] A martial arts teacher.

I was checking on a child in the hospital who was having a rough time of it. The nursing staff said that he had stopped talking a few days ago and wouldn't even make eye contact. His primary doctor asked me to look in on him.

He stared out the window as soon as I entered the room. I sat by his bed for a few minutes. He watched my reflection in the glass.

"I went to my doctor today," I said as I lowered my eyes and started to play with my own fingers. My wife thinks I'm fat. She isn't mean or nothing. I don't know why she thinks that. But she does, she thinks I'm fat."

"Really? How come you had to go to the doctor?" he turned and looked at me.

"Oh, I'm OK but I had to have a check up. I didn't even have to get any shots this time," I smiled.

"The doctor gave me a huge bottle of pills," I said as I showed with my arms a laundry basket size bottle. "It was filled with 500 pills the size of baseballs. So, I told him I can't swallow a horse pill and he couldn't make me!"

"Wow," the wide eyed little patient agreed.

"You don't have to," he said, "all you have to do is pour them out everyday and pick each of them up. You need the exercise."

The little boy smiled knowing I was pulling his leg.

Then we were able to talk about being poked and prodded, and the importance of it all. He was an amazingly caring soul.

A few days later when I checked back in on the boy the first thing he said was, "I've been worried about you, have you been picking up your horse pills?" He had a stern look on his face with a slight smile.

I told him, "No. But I have been walking with Big Dog and he is almost the size of a horse."

"You should check with the doctor if that is the same as picking up the pills. You have to do what the doctor says if you want to get better," he said as he patted my hand gently.

623. ☆ ☆ ☆ ☆ ☆ ☆ ☆ ☆ ☆

Play nice

My brother Garry and I were on the way to our sister's home for dinner. We made a pact that no matter what Diane said, it was her house and we were not going to get in any stupid arguments. We bolstered our resolve, "She is nice enough to cook a wonderful dinner for us, we should be mature enough not to be rude and argue with her, no matter what!" We vowed to ourselves, "No politics and no family gossip." Our goal was to be the prefect dinner guests.

Well, as you can imagine, we had had experiences with Diane that led to arguments. In our defense, Diane was really good at getting upset over very minor things.

Diane met us at the door with her little tea cup poodle, Sir Lancelot. As part of our plan Garry and I were going to lavish affection on Sir Lancelot hoping to garner points with our sister.

"There he is, you look so cute. You're such a smart fellow," we repeated.

Diane ate it up. She stood in the doorway letting us praise the little ball of black curly fuzz.

"You look so cute. You're such a smart little doggie." I said as I picked him up.

Talking right at his fluffy face I gushed praise upon him. Garry backed me up, as my praise wingman.

As Diane turned away from the door she said, "Don't be such a pest Lanceeepoo, let the boys come in."

At that very moment, Lanceeepoo's face wagged and I realized that I had been talking to his bum the whole time.

It has been 20 years and we have never told Diane this story. So mum's the word.

624. ☆ ☆ ☆ ☆ ☆ ☆ ☆ ☆ ☆

The poker game

The week I graduated from grad school, my friends threw me a poker game to celebrate. Back in the day, we didn't play for winnings as we were all broke. We played for bragging rights. On a really good night you could maybe— be up or down— $20. As the night wore on I was having a very good night. The cards were falling in my favor as if I had stacked the deck.

After a particularly feisty Acey-Deucey game, where the pot got out of control, I walked away with a huge sum of $140.

My friend Mike, who was way past drunk, slurred at me, "You asssssshoooool!"

To which I replied, "That's Dr. Asshole to you!"

625. ☆☆☆☆☆☆☆☆☆

Flat broke in Reno

Another story from grad school days is about my oldest friend Gust.

He had gone to Reno for a weekend of fun, but the tables were not kind to him. He was down to his last $40 dollars. To make sure he got home, he went to his car and put a $20 bill in the glove compartment, enough for gas. Then he went back to win his fortune with his last 20.

He lost everything, so he filled up his tank in Reno, Nevada and headed back to San Jose, California without a penny in his pocket.

All was going fine until he read a sign, "Toll Booth Ahead 1/2 Mile". He had forgotten about the bridge toll. He needed $2.

He pulled off the highway and searched his glove compartment. Nothing. He checked the trunk of his car and found 79¢ in his dirty laundry. He decided that the toll bridge people must have a way for him to pay later, so he got back into his car thinking about how stupid it was not to have 2 bucks!

When he went to start his car, he realized that he had locked his keys in the trunk. He ended up having to take out the back seat to break into his own trunk.

Finally, he had his keys and he was off to ask for help from the toll booth operator.

Thirty seconds later he turned the curve in the highway to read another sign: Free Direction.

For years after this, whenever he would stop abruptly, his back seat would dislodge and fall forward. His Plymouth Fury never let Gust forget the indignity of that day.

626.   ☆ ☆ ☆ ☆ ☆ ☆ ☆ ☆ ☆

Fun with words

My beloved, Geri sent me this email. She has been my editor for 2 decades and enjoys teasing me for my notorious misspellings:

From NPR Science Friday:

OCDRNDICG TO RSCHEEARCH AT CMABRIGDE UINERVTISY, IT DSENO'T MTAETR WAHT OERDR THE LTTERES IN A WROD ARE, THE OLNY IPROAMTNT TIHNG IS TAHT THE FRSIT AND LSAT LTTEER BE IN THE RGHIT PCLAE. TIHS IS BCUSEAE THE HUAMN MNID DEOS NOT RAED ERVEY LTETER BY ISTLEF, BUT THE WROD AS A WLOHE. IF YOU CAN

RAED TIHS, PSOT IT TO YUOR WLAL. OLNY 55% OF PLEPOE CAN.

So, where do you fit in?

My response:

Hi Grie,

No peblorm raenidg tihs, it is how I nrolalmy sepll.

Lvoe,

PC

627.

The royal wedding

When Prince William and Catherine Middleton were married it was an international event. People in my area were having Royal Wedding parties that started at 10 PM and went all night long so that they could watch the proceedings live on TV.

I personally had no interest in the festivities even though I wish them well. I did have one thought, however. I wondered if after the wedding and the parties, when the world knew that the newlyweds were all settled into bed, if millions of people would be running around in the streets yelling, "The British are coming! The British are coming!"

I hope so.

"Well Rabbi Bobby, I learned not to eat the calamari at the bris."

628. ☆ ☆ ☆ ☆ ☆ ☆ ☆ ☆ ☆

Gust's brother

I met my friend, Gust, in graduate school. I was really poor and he had an empty couch which he let me use on a regular basis. Gust lived with his brother and one other student. Frequently Gust's brother, Mike would bring home girls. I'm not exaggerating this. Mike was a girl magnet. He would go to the store to buy anything and bring back an amazingly attractive coed. Mike also seemed very honest with these girls. He would invite them over for sex and then politely ask them to go.

Some nights Mike would have three different ladies over— 6, 8 and 10 PM dates. He would bed them and then send them on their way. Over the years we rarely saw the same girl twice.

On this particular night, Gust and I were studying in the livingroom when loud moans began to emanate from upstairs. Over the next 30 minutes the moans were unbelievably loud.

Gust and I tried to block the moans out. Soon we were simply starring at the ceiling in amazement. After 10 minutes we were laughing. By the time the moans stopped, we were laughing uncontrollably.

As we heard Mike and his guest starting down the stairs Gust said, "We've got to pull ourselves together." We tried our best and were pretending to be studying when Mike politely introduced us to his date, "Hi guys, I want you to meet Mona."

Three days later I was still unable to take a full breath because I pulled stomach and rib muscles laughing convulsively.

629. ☆ ☆ ☆ ☆ ☆ ☆ ☆ ☆

Saturn and the girlfriend's new bird

One point in college I lived in a huge dumpy house with three German Shepard dogs, Satan, Saturn, and Dillinger. All three were super friendly.

Saturn was like a hyperactive dog on methamphetamine. I'm not kidding, this was one active puppy.

One day my girlfriend showed up with a present. A parakeet in a small metal cage. She thought I needed a pet parakeet.

Because of the dogs, we decided to place the cage high in the large doorway between the living-room and the dining-room. I don't want you to get the wrong idea about this house. It may have had a living-room and a dining-room but by name only. The landlord bought the house from the city for $75 on the assumption that he would fix it up and start to pay taxes on it. I got to live in the place for almost nothing as long as I kept the squatters out until he got around to fixing it up. The only heat in the building came from the three dogs.

My girlfriend wanted to introduce the dogs to the bird slowly. First Satan, then Dillinger, then lastly Saturn. Satan and Dillinger could care less about a cage hanging between the dining-room and the living-room.

Saturn was amazingly curious. She ran into the dining-room, sat beneath the cage, and then bounced up six feet to look into the cage. Then again from a sitting position she bounced up to look into the cage. The bird didn't know what was going on. The third time Saturn bounced up we heard a hard thud. The little birdie probably had a heart attack, fell off its perch and THUD, landed on the cage floor.

We never even got to name the bird, so other than the empty cage, we never talked about it again. My girlfriend never brought me another live gift after that. She brought me baked goods or fast food. It was probably better that way.

After I graduated and needed to move to California for grad school, my girlfriend kept Saturn. They bonded through the tragedy, which is the way it goes so often.

630. ☆ ☆ ☆ ☆ ☆ ☆ ☆ ☆

Tommy the tortoise

To the big house on Garson Avenue came a visitor. My brother Garry asked me to babysit for his tortoise, Tommy. Tommy was a cool creature about the size of a cantaloupe. He was easy to watch over. He roamed about the dining-room and the living-room happily for months. Then spring came, and Satan thought that the rock with legs needed to be buried in the backyard. He was down right sneaky about it. I never saw him do it. I would notice dirt on his snout and a fresh mound in the backyard.

Tommy seemed OK with the indignity. When I would disinter him he didn't seem to care. I'd rinse him off in the sink and set him free to frolic around the house.

Unfortunately, one day I didn't realize that Satan had buried Tommy in a shallow grave. The snow covered the deed. When I realized what had happened and found Tommy... it was too late. The poor fellow had frozen to death.

Initially I was going to bury him and then call Garry with the bad news. But burying Tommy seemed somehow dreadfully wrong. So I put him in the freezer and waited for Garry to return in a few weeks. I figured he would want to say his last goodbyes.

I took Tommy out of the freezer the day I was to pick up Garry at the airport. I placed him on a towel on the kitchen table and tried to make the scene look dignified. Like a viewing at a mortuary. I used the maroon kitchen towel because it looked most regal. Tommy looked to be sleeping in his protective shell.

On the drive from the airport I told Garry about the "incident" between Tommy and Satan. Incident sounded so much better than "murder". Garry was upset but understanding. He was kind enough not to bring up, as proof of my poor pet sitting skills, the incident with the girlfriend's bird. That incident now is referred to as, *the thud heard around the house.*

When we got to my place Garry went in first. Garry was immediately mad at me. "That's not funny, Tommy's alive."

"What?" I said.

I looked at Tommy and his head and legs were out of his shell. His eyes were open. He looked like he was trying to walk on the maroon kitchen towel.

Unfortunately, Tommy was still dead. As he warmed up his body must have fermented and made him puff out. We buried him in the backyard before he exploded.

631. ☆ ☆ ☆ ☆ ☆ ☆ ☆ ☆

Mountain Man

My family and I live in the woods far off the beaten path in northern California. My closest neighbors are a phone call away and my mountain is full of majestic black oaks and 200 year old ponderosa pines.

Our long driveway takes us to a windy country road. From there it is still another 5 miles to the closest town. The tiny town consists of a post office, small public school, and a bar.

One of our neighbors turned their home into a bed and breakfast. So, from time to time you would pass someone on the country road who was from Sacramento or San Francisco. Their fancy cars stuck out among the trucks and economical runabouts that frequent my little part of the world.

One cold winter morning my wife, Geri, woke me up and told me that she and the kids couldn't get to school because a large pine tree had fallen across the county road just below the end of the driveway.

I got dressed for the cold and took the truck down the driveway and went about the business of carving up the mid section of the tree that blocked the road.

About halfway through the chore, a large white Cadillac drove down from the bed and breakfast and stopped a short distance away. Three older ladies ended up standing by their car watching me. It was a funny sight. The were dressed grandly, wearing party dresses, jewels, heels, and mink coats.

About a half hour later, as I was cutting the last part of the tree that was blocking the road, there was a flash of light that bounced off the snow and caught my attention. As I looked up, one lady said to the other, "Maybe it's not polite to take his picture."

The photographer said, "But, I've never seen a real mountain man before."

I smiled at them and rolled the last section of log off the road.

As the Caddie drove by, the ladies smiled and waved goodbye to me.

I drove back to the house to get ready for work. On my way into the city of Redding, as I drove by the fallen tree, I realized that I was turning from mountain man into Dr. Phil.

"Polly view français?"

632.   ☆ ☆ ☆ ☆ ☆ ☆ ☆ ☆ ☆ ☆

The bug man in the lady's bedroom

I have a friend who is an exterminator. He is quite scientific in his approach and has spent a career solving homeowners' pest issues. He also has a few stories to tell:

"I was spraying pesticide around the interior of a house. I have worked for this lady for years. She was a grandma type who always offered me a soft drink or a cup of tea.

"When I got to the master bedroom, I inadvertently sprayed something under the head of the bed. When I realized it was a very large double ended purple dildo, I got really nervous.

"I couldn't pretend that I didn't spray it, that could be very dangerous. I could just tell her about it, but that would be too uncomfortable. So I grabbed it and rushed to the bathroom and washed it with hot soapy water. After I dried it, I returned it under the bed, away from where I had sprayed.

"I was never so uncomfortable as when I was washing that thing. It was huge and had veins. I had a hard time getting all the soap off of it. What if she asked me what I was doing?

633. ☆ ☆ ☆ ☆ ☆ ☆ ☆ ☆ ☆

The bug man on the back porch

My friend the bug man tells a story about the time when he peed off his back porch:

"I live in the country. My closest neighbor is a quarter mile away. So here I am peeing off the back porch at 2 o'clock in the morning. It's pitch black, when all of a sudden my pee is glowing yellow. I realize that there's a flashlight focused on my thing!

"Sorry," the lady next door said, "have you seen my dog?"

We both pretend it never happened.

634. ☆ ☆ ☆ ☆ ☆ ☆ ☆ ☆ ☆

Out of the mouth of babes

When my son Ethan was 7 years old we watched a Bill Cosby skit where the comic line was, "You have another think coming!" For days Ethan was saying, "You have another think coming!"

Shortly after that his little brother Josh came running into the kitchen to tell on him. Ethan was furious. He ran into the kitchen to stop him and screamed, "You have another <u>fink</u> coming!"

635. ☆ ☆ ☆ ☆ ☆ ☆ ☆ ☆ ☆

Me and golf

I am regularly invited to play golf, and people always seem surprised when I tell them that I don't play the game. I borrowed a one liner from Jack Benny. When asked if I play golf I say, "Ah, golf… give me fresh air, my golf clubs, and my beautiful wife… and you can keep the fresh air and golf clubs. I'd rather go to brunch Sunday morning with my wife."

But the truth is, and please do not judge me too harshly, I have played golf a few times and found it boring. My sport is JuJitsu. An active sport. Punch, kick, break stuff. Hopefully their stuff. In golf, I hit the ball and I have to go get it myself. Why? If I wanted the damn ball, why did I hit it way over there?

I once had a patient tell me about her husband, "He'll spend 30 minutes looking for a golf ball, but in 10 years of marriage he has never spent 3 minutes looking for my g-spot!"

The last time I played golf I really hurt myself. I was being coached by a friend and I did what he said. "Eye on the ball, knees bent, swing though the ball." I hit a grass clog 20 feet and wrenched my shoulder. I couldn't do JuJitsu for weeks. Golf is dangerous. I'm sticking to martial arts.

636. ☆ ☆ ☆ ☆ ☆ ☆ ☆ ☆ ☆

When my mom first met my fiancée

When my mother and my soon to be wife first met, I knew I was in trouble. My mother liked Geri instantaneously. Near the end of our visit, my mother doled out some motherly advice, "Geri, Philip is a nice boy, but you can do better."

I happen to agree and regularly tell Geri so.

637. ☆ ☆ ☆ ☆ ☆ ☆ ☆ ☆ ☆

Did God live in 5C?

My mother and her twin sister Rosa tended to get along well. One particular day, my little brother, Garry, and I came home from school and walked into the apartment which was engulfed in the emotional flames of anger.

My mother was being accused of lying, and my aunt was screaming about how hurt she was about being treated in such a way.

My mother was furious and said in Yiddish, "On the heads of my children I am telling the truth."

With this, Aunt Rosa straightened herself up, got back her composure, and left the house without a word.

I looked at my little brother who asked, "What did mom just say?"

"Mom just said that were going to die." I said.

"How come?"

"Because I know mom was lying, and if I know, I think God knows."

Garry pondered this for a moment, "Everyone knows but Aunt Rosa."

On a side note, I never did understand how come old people in my family would regularly evoke the All Mighty and barter using us kids as collateral. My mother would say things like, "On the eyes of my children..." or "May God strike my children dead if..."

If, as a child, you were being too loud or obnoxious you would hear, "Strashen net de genz" which literally means, "do not disturb the geese". I would think, "Geese? Where are these geese?"

Often, when my mother was upset with us kids she would talk directly to God. She would make a fist and punch the air with anger as she explained to God that she did not deserve children that caused such troubles. She would ask, "Vos iz di chochmeh?" Meaning "What is the wisdom?"

For a while we lived in apartment 4C. A very old man lived in apartment 5C directly above us. One time, when mom was arguing with God... I wondered if this old man was God? He was old enough. But he walked with a cane. Would God need a cane? I knew he didn't speak English, so yelling at the ceiling in Yiddish kind of made sense. I wasn't sure if he was God, but I was always very nice to him just in case.

"Your Holiness, you put your fingers together like this and this is how you build the church."

638. ☆ ☆ ☆ ☆ ☆ ☆ ☆ ☆ ☆

Dr. Phil I thought you were gay

I had been working with this couple for three weeks when I brought up that my wife and I were expecting our second child. The couple asked me how hard it was for my partner and my wife to get along. After a few awkward moments, I figured out what was going on and explained that I wasn't gay, and that my wife was named Geri, short for Geraldine.

The couple I was working with were gay and assumed I was also, since I worked with gay couples. At the end of the session, one of the men smiled and said to me, "For a breeder, you make a very good gay therapist."

Punning along I said, "For my age, I make a very good child therapist too."

639. ☆ ☆ ☆ ☆ ☆ ☆ ☆ ☆ ☆

Friday Night Live

I once played softball on the mental health team for the county I worked for. We were by far the worst team in the league. But we were also skilled at helping ourselves feel OK about sucking so badly. When we played the police department it was embarrassing. The fire department was even worse. Let's put it this way, we really helped every other team's stats.

We were invited to play the local Alcoholics Anonymous team. We were told that they were fun and didn't take the game too seriously.

They met on Friday nights and played under the lights. The idea was to keep their members active on a potentially troublesome night. The AA team was fun and amazingly supportive. They cheered for each other and even for us. Their enthusiasm was wonderful to see.

Late in the game, it was my turn at bat. I was usually good for a single but, to my surprise, I really got a piece of the ball and it sailed over the outfielder's head. I was running to second and my third base coach was waving me to third. I was huffing and puffing and he signaled me to slide.

"Slide!" I thought, you don't slide into first base. I only ever get to first base. But, I did it. Like a graceful walrus I slid.

"Out!" yelled the umpire.

I was pissed. I really wanted to hit a triple. I grumped at myself and this man came over to me. "It's OK, you tried your best," he said.

"Ah, that was stupid I should have stayed on second," I growled.

"It's OK," he said gently. "It all doesn't matter, as long as we alcoholics don't drink."

Not thinking about what he was saying I grunted, "I'm not an alcoholic!"

My kind new friend lost it on me. He screamed at the top of his lungs, "It's going to be all OK. It's just a game! Drinking is not the answer! Is your sponsor here? Think about your family..."

At this point I figured out what was going on and thanked him for his love. I promised him I wouldn't drink. He gave me a big hug and told me as he trotted off, "Keep the faith brother. Keep the faith."

I don't know who that man was but I surely am glad that I got to meet him.

640. ☆ ☆ ☆ ☆ ☆ ☆ ☆ ☆

Ducks in the bathtub and goldfish in the toilet

My friend the dentist built himself a new home in the woods. Even though it was off the beaten path, this new house had all the luxuries. A pool with a babbling rock waterfall, amazing vista of Shasta Lake, and a master bathroom with sunken Jacuzzi tub and separate fancy massage shower. The bathroom alone was larger than my first apartment.

I teased my friend that the bathtub was so deep that he was going to drown, unable to get out of it.

After the house was complete and my friend was comfortably moved in I bought two large white ducks and a few hundred goldfish. The plan was to sneak the ducks into the bathtub. That way, when my friend got home, he would hear "quacks" and eventually find the ducks. The goldfish went into the toilet tanks. So, after he flushed the toilet, goldfish would miraculously show up in the toilet bowl.

When he accused me of the prank I denied everything. He said, "I heard ducks and didn't know what was going on. 'Did a duck get in through an open window?' I followed the noise and was pretty sure that the duck was in the bathroom. I opened the door. No duck. I closed the door and heard quacks and fluttering. I open the door, no duck. This went on a few times and I thought "There must be someone hiding in the tub messing with me. So I opened the door and yelled in. Nothing. Then two duck heads peeked up out of the bathtub."

At this point, I was howling with laughter.

"It wasn't funny!" my friend said. "The ducks were scared. They shit everywhere. The tub was full of shit. I had to grab them and carry them out of the house. They didn't want to be grabbed. They pecked at me and shit even more. Projectile shit! It isn't funny!"

"When I got back from the lake, I had to clean up the bathroom, the hall, the stairs, the downstairs hall, the porch, and my truck. I finally was ready for a shower. I peed. Damn! Goldfish!"

I was hurting myself laughing so hard, and still denying everything.

"It's not funny. I still have fish in my toilets. They don't want to go down. You flush and they swim up stream like salmon."

"You touch 600 people an hour, but you're always too tired for me!"

641.

Very depressed

Many years ago, I was working with a brilliant patient who was very depressed. She told me that she was a horrible person and that she deserved all the horrible things that happened to her. She was sure that she deserved even more horrible things. She spoke in a slow and deliberate monotone while staring at her feet. She unloaded her self hate until her pain filled the room.

"I deserve to get cancer and slowly die. I deserve to have my flesh slowly rot off my body and to decay from the inside out..."

This type of talk continued for 20 minutes. She finished her slow sad monologue by saying, "I deserve to have an AIDS infected midget rape me in unspeakable ways. So I can suffer a painfully slow death from AIDS."

"Why a midget?" I asked.

"Because," she continued coldly, "I don't even deserve a good fuck."

"Well dear, would you like anything from the comfort cart... blanket, gown, oxygen mask, morphine drip? If you have Blue Cross I can let you have a pillow for 18 percent off!"

6. Jokes my wife forbade me from telling again

My bride of almost 25 years tends to have a good sense of humor. Most of the time she puts up with my jokes and antics. On a few occasions she has even participated with my practical jokes.

On a rare occasion, when I tell a joke that she perceives as tawdry, she will call me by my complete first name, "Philip!" and indicate with a look of motherly distain how disappointed she is in my choices. I assume she expects me to refrain from telling the offending joke again.

I have noticed that my beloved does not like jokes with particular scenarios and/or words in them. She dislikes the "C" word and does not appreciate any story concerning cavernous vaginal areas or lost items in said areas.

But the truth be told, she tends to laugh at this type of joke just before she says, "Philip!"

If you are offended by such humor, you may wish to skip to Chapter 7.

642.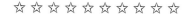

Stanley and Sylvia are a nice Jewish couple who have been married for 46 years.

Sylvia calls from the toilet.

"Stanley, come quick!"

"What happened?" he says as he runs into the bathroom.

"I think a mouse ran up my leg and into my unmentionable!"

"Oh my God, this can't be good," Stanley says. "I better call the doctor."

Stanley rushes off and calls the doctor then he returns to his Sylvia, who is not so happy.

"Sylvia, the doctor said he is coming right over but it is going to take about twenty minutes. He suggested that we should try to bribe the mouse out with a little cheese. What do you think we should do?"

"This isn't happening to me!" Sylvia cries. "Get the cheese."

The doctor finally arrives and he walks into the bathroom. To his surprise he finds Sylvia sitting on the toilet and Stanley on his knees waving a pickled herring around between Sylvia's legs.

"Stanley, what are you doing! I told you to use cheese to get the mouse out!"

"I know, I know, I wasn't born yesterday! But first I got to get the cat out!"

643. ☆ ☆ ☆ ☆ ☆ ☆ ☆ ☆ ☆ ☆

My Aunt Hilda was talking to the nice Irish lady down the hall.

"So I noticed your Miles brought you flowers last night," Hilda pried.

"Oh yes, Miles is very good to me. Last night, he was so romantic," she said.

"Me, I don't care for flowers," Hilda confessed.

"Really, how come?"

"When my Morris brings me flowers, it means, you know," she lowered her voice. "He wants me to spread my legs and put my feet up into the air."

"How come, Hilda?" the nice Irish lady asked. "Don't you have a vase?"

644.   ☆ ☆ ☆ ☆ ☆ ☆ ☆ ☆ ☆

My Uncle Monty met this nice girl, Sarah, through the Jewish singles group. They dated for a few weeks when finally she invited him back to her place.

As the evening progressed, and the wine was flowing freely, she confessed that she had a very talented nether region. After a little more coaxing and a little more wine, Sarah explained that her unmentionable could sing.

"Sing?" Uncle Monty repeated.

"Yes it can sing, let me show you."

And she did just that. She sat on the couch showing everything she had. But that wasn't the amazing thing. Sarah's madam wonderful sang well. For hours it sang opera, show tunes, and even holiday ditties.

Uncle Monty was so impressed he had tears in his eyes from the beauty of the rendition.

Then he got an idea.

"Sarah, I got a friend in show business. A big time producer. Let me call him and you can sing for him. You'll be rich. You'll be famous."

So Uncle Monty dialed the phone and his friend answered, "Hello."

"Harvey listen to this."

Uncle Monty put the phone between Sarah's legs, and after the song was over, Uncle Monty said, "Harvey what do you think?"

Harvey was furious, "You woke me up at 3 in the morning just to have some dumb cunt sing 'Hello Dolly'!"

645. ☆☆☆☆☆☆☆☆☆☆

How do you know when a prostitute is full?
Her nose is running.

646. ☆☆☆☆☆☆☆☆☆☆

Larry comes home and finds his wife of three years crying on the bed.
"What's wrong sweetie?" Larry asked.
"I'm so mad at you Larry!" she snarls. "I found out today that

you're a pedophile!"

"A pedophile!" Larry protested. "That's an awfully big word for a 10-year-old."

647. ☆ ☆ ☆ ☆ ☆ ☆ ☆ ☆ ☆

How do you perform an Ozark vasectomy?
Kick the man's daughter really hard in the jaw.

648. ☆ ☆ ☆ ☆ ☆ ☆ ☆ ☆ ☆

A man walked into a bar and sat down at the far end of the counter. The bartender takes a look at him and then does a double take. Over the next few minutes the bartender finds himself taking quick, uncomfortable glances at the man.

The bartender brings the man a beer and says apologetically, "I'm sorry mister. Staring like that is really rude of me. This beer's on the house. But I just can't seem to stop looking at you. I don't want to be mean," the bartender continues, "but you must be the ugliest man I have ever seen."

"Yeah, I hear that a lot, but the ladies love me," the ugly man says.

"Really? But..." The bartender stops himself.

"Yeah really!" the ugly man says. "I'll bet you $50 I can get any woman you pick in this place to go home with me!"

The bartender slaps fifty dollars on the counter and points to the corner table. "That young lady over there with the handsome boyfriend."

"Sure," said the ugly man. "In fact, I'll bet you another 50 I can smack her on the ass as we walk out of here and she'll squeal with joy and even wink at you because she will be so excited about leaving with me!"

"You've got to be kidding," the bartender said as he slapped another $50 on the counter.

The ugly man got up and walked back to the attractive couple at the corner table. In a few seconds the young woman is apologizing to her date and heading out the door with the ugly man. As they pass the bartender, the ugly man swats the gorgeous woman on her perfect bottom and she giggles and hugs his arm as she flashes a sexy wink at the bartender. The ugly man grabs the money and they leave.

The bartender is really confused. He goes over to the corner table and speaks to the befuddled handsome man. "That ugly man, what did he say to your date?"

"He didn't say anything. He just stood there licking his eyebrows."

649. ☆ ☆ ☆ ☆ ☆ ☆ ☆ ☆ ☆

A drunk finds a crisp new twenty dollar bill and thinks to himself, "I haven't had sex for a while."

So the drunk goes to the local house of ill repute and asks what he can get for $20.

The madam says, "For $20 you can have Old Thelma for 15 minutes."

At the end of it all the drunk was happy and thanked the madam for her hospitality.

"We're here to oblige, your money is always good here," the madam says as the drunk goes out the door.

A few days later, the drunk finds a shiny new fifty-cent piece. Thinking of the good time at the whorehouse he decides to see what he can get for half a buck.

"Sure," the madam says while taking the coin, "we can accommodate you honey." Then she hollers down the basement stairs, "Hey Charlie, grease up the cat."

650. ☆☆☆☆☆☆☆☆

A naked lady gets into a cab and says, "42nd Street."

"Hey lady," says the cab driver, "how are you going to pay, you don't even have a purse?"

"I'm going to pay you with this!" she said as she pointed to her madam wonderful.

"Come on lady, don't you have anything smaller?"

651. ☆☆☆☆☆☆☆☆

Melvin was really down on his luck but wanted sex really badly. He had heard through a friend that down an ally off of Fifth and Bourbon was a whorehouse that would satisfy you no matter how little money you had.

"I only have $20," Melvin told the burly man that policed the entrance.

"For $20 you get to go down to room 6 and you'll figure out what to do," the burly man grunted.

Melvin went to room 6. Inside he found a chicken. Figuring "what the hell," he had his way with the fowl. To his surprise he got into the act and enjoyed himself immensely.

Over the next few days, Melvin found himself getting randier and randier. He only had a dollar, but he approached the burly man.

"Can I get any action for a buck?" Melvin asked.

"For a buck," the burly man snarled, "you don't get to touch. You get to go to room 9, you'll figure out what to do."

Room 9 was a dark long hallway. Men were sitting on stools and peeping through holes in the wall. Melvin found an empty stool and watched a fat man have sex with an old lady."

When the show was over, Marvin said to the guy next to him, "That wasn't too bad."

The other man said, "You should've been here last week, there was a guy in there with a chicken."

652. ☆ ☆ ☆ ☆ ☆ ☆ ☆ ☆ ☆

Pierre emigrated from France to America with his family when he was 16 years old. It was very difficult at first. He worked hard and he learned the American customs of business. By his early thirties he was wealthy, and in his fifties he was financially set for life.

At this point he decided to go back to France and buy the villa his father had been a laborer at when he was a small boy. He and his wife made the trip together. While walking around the luscious grounds he had a rush of wonderful memories.

"Honey," he told his wife, "that was the tree I told you about. The one that I sat under when I tended to the sheep. I would sit in its shade for hours looking over this beautiful landscape."

As they walked he continued. "That tree over there was where I had sex for the very first time. We were there while her mother was lounging under that tree over there." He pointed.

"Her mother? But she would have seen everything. What did she say?"

"Baaahh."

"Who's your farmer?"

653. ☆ ☆ ☆ ☆ ☆ ☆ ☆ ☆

Why do men in Red Bluff like to have sex with their sheep high up on the bluffs overlooking the valley?

When the sheep are scared they push back.

7. In closing, my favorite jokes

I am constantly asked what is my favorite joke. This is a tough question because it depends on my mood and the audience. Please don't judge me too harshly, but here are my favorite jokes.

If you don't laugh heartily as you read these, maybe you're dead or you can't read.

"I think I'm retaining pizza."

654. ☆ ☆ ☆ ☆ ☆ ☆ ☆ ☆ ☆ ☆

Mr. Grossman was visiting Mumbai, India on a business trip when he was in a terrible car accident. The engine ended up in his lap and he was lucky to survive. After he came out of the coma the doctors explained that due to the extensive damage they had to replace his manhood with a baby elephant's trunk.

Mr. Grossman was so happy to be alive he decide to just go home and get follow up care in New York.

When he got to his doctor's office, his doctor asked him how the new trunk was working for him. Mr. Grossman said, "Overall not too bad. It seems to have a mind of its own though. Last night I was out at a restaurant and as the waiter walked by with a basket of hot bread, my trunk reached up out of the top of my pants and stole a whole loaf of French bread."

"Interesting," said the doctor. "Any other complications? Any pain?"

"Oh yeah doc," said Mr. Grossman. "It was really painful when my trunk shoved that hot loaf of bread up my ass!"

655.   ☆ ☆ ☆ ☆ ☆ ☆ ☆ ☆ ☆

The circus came to Red Bluff. In keeping with tradition, to announce the arrival of the circus, they paraded their acts down Main Street. There were acrobats and the Fat Lady, along with tall clowns on stilts juggling balls and bowling pins. The highlight of the event was the elephants. Everyone came to see the giant pachyderms walk nose to tail down Main Street.

The first enormous elephant was leading the others. The next elephant held the biggest elephant's tail. In this fashion, nose to tail, each elephant got a little smaller. The last elephant was a baby, and it was so cute it was stealing the show. It held the tail of the elephant in front of it, while it wagged its head and seemed to be enjoying the attention.

Barreling into town was the 4:15 from Sacramento. A long freight train of over fifty boxcars. The engineer saw the elephants starting to cross the tracks and did everything he could. But there was no way to stop the train from hitting the lead elephant.

When the train finally stopped, the engineer ran back to the fallen elephant. The engineer was heart broken and said to the elephant trainer, "I'm so sorry mister. It was all my fault, I was running behind so I was going too fast through town. I'm sure the train company will buy you a new elephant."

"A new elephant! I want ten new elephants!" yelled the trainer.

"Ten? But I only killed one!"

"Yeah, but you pulled the assholes out of nine others!"

656.   ☆ ☆ ☆ ☆ ☆ ☆ ☆ ☆ ☆

Tony went to China on a business trip. His last night there he got really drunk and couldn't quite remember what happened. A few days later, back at home he noticed that his manhood was not looking so good. He went to one doctor, then to another. He was horrified when the third doctor told him the same thing, they would have to amputate.

Out of desperation Tony thinks, "Chinese girl, maybe a Chinese doctor can help." So he goes to Chinatown and goes down some steps and knocks on the red satin curtain.

"You come in," said Dr. Chang. "What problem is?"

Tony is too nervous to speak, so he just drops his pants.

"Dr. Chang knows what problem is. You come to right place. Dr. Chang will help."

"Oh thank God," Tony blurts. "The American doctors were no help at all."

"American doctor told you they have to amputate?"

"Yeah," said Tony.

"American doctor say they have to cut off your dick?" Dr. Chang said as he shook his head. "No, no, no, you don't have too cut off your dick."

"Thank heavens," said Tony.

"Sure. In two, three days, it fall off by self."

657. ☆ ☆ ☆ ☆ ☆ ☆ ☆ ☆ ☆

When my Uncle Monty and Aunt Sadie immigrated from the old country they lived in Chicago. They didn't have much money so they ended up in a cheap one room apartment under an elevated train station. That first night, all night long the trains went by and Aunt Sadie was bounced out of bed. The next day, when Uncle Monty was out looking for work, Aunt Sadie told the building superintendent about the problem with the train.

He said, "I never heard of such a thing."

So Aunt Sadie took him back to her room and made him lie on the bed with her.

Just then, Uncle Monty came home, "Hey, what's going on here?"

"To tell you the truth," Aunt Sadie said, "I'm waiting for a train."

658. ☆ ☆ ☆ ☆ ☆ ☆ ☆ ☆ ☆

When I was a little kid I saw two dogs doing something in the park. Now, I know what they were doing, but back then I had no idea what was going on. So I asked my Uncle Sol.

"The one in the front is ill and the one in the back is pushing him to Mount Sinai Hospital," Uncle Sol told me.

I didn't know that Uncle Sol was lying, so a few years later, when I was eight, I saw two men behind a bush at the park doing the same thing. I thought of the dogs. With all the moaning I was pretty sure the one in front was hurt and the one behind needed help. So I went to help.

"Help, help!" I yelled. "We need help to get this man to Mount Sinai Hospital!"

They beat the shit out of me.

Again, I went and asked my Uncle what was going on.

"You see bubelah," Uncle Sol said. "Those two are what they call the gay. Don't worry about it anymore, get some ice for your head and go do your homework."

I sat in my room with an ice pack on my head, and for the first time in my life I figured out that Uncle Sol lied to me. I was positive that those two men were not happy. They were pissed. They beat the shit out of me!

659. ☆ ☆ ☆ ☆ ☆ ☆ ☆ ☆ ☆ ☆

A small church put an ad in their local paper for a bell ringer. Because of the low pay and hourly schedule the parish priest was expecting to have a hard time finding a new bell ringer. When the priest ascended to the bell tower, it was worse than he expected. There was only one applicant, and he had no arms.

"I'm here for the bell ringer job," the armless man said enthusiastically.

"But," the priest stated, "how can you ring the bell?"

"No problem," said the man. And without another word he took a run at the bell, hitting it hard with his whole body.

"Ding," went the bell.

The armless man got to his feet, his nose was bleeding, and his eyes were all puffy. The priest said to him, "Good try my child, but that wasn't nearly loud enough."

The man went to the far side of the belfry and ran hard at the bell. Just before hitting it, the man stumbled and completely missed the bell——falling out of the belfry and down to the ground below.

The priest rushed down the bell tower steps. A crowd had already formed. It was obvious to all that the man was a goner. A policeman said to the priest, "Father, do you know this poor fellow's name?"

Shaking his head with sorrow, the priest said, "No, but his face rings a bell."

660. ☆ ☆ ☆ ☆ ☆ ☆ ☆ ☆ ☆ ☆

Knock Knock!
Who's there?
Is
Is who?
No no, it's correct to say, "Is whom."

661. ☆ ☆ ☆ ☆ ☆ ☆ ☆ ☆ ☆ ☆

How do you sell a chicken to a deaf man?

Hold the chicken up and yell! "DO YOU WANT TO BUY A CHICKEN!"

"I'm looking for an autobiography of a caveman."

When you tell this joke you have to sell it by yelling loudly and dramatically shaking an imaginary chicken.

662. ☆ ☆ ☆ ☆ ☆ ☆ ☆ ☆ ☆

When my Uncle Sol and Uncle Monty escaped from the Nazis at the beginning of World War II they ended up in France. In no time they had to get out of France, so they went to Rome, Italy. Their goal was to make enough money to get to America.

Times were hard, and without proper papers it was impossible to find work. So Uncle Sol and Uncle Monty had no choice but to beg on the streets.

Uncle Sol was sitting in front of the Vatican with his hat on the ground and a sign, *Please Help a Jew to get to America*, when a kindly older priest came over to talk to him.

"I see by your sign and your clothes that you are a poor Jew." the priest said gently.

"Yes, that is so," said Uncle Sol.

"I don't want to be rude, but you do know that you are sitting in front of the Vatican, the holiest place in all of Christendom?" asked the priest.

"Yes, I know," nodded Uncle Sol.

"You do know that everyone that comes here are good Christians?"

"Yes, I suppose so."

"You do know that you are sitting next to a man with a sign that reads, *Christian - Please Help.*"

"Yes, that is so," said Uncle Sol.

"Have you noticed that the Christian has a hat full of money and your hat is almost empty?" said the kind priest. "It makes sense that Christians would rather give to their own people. In fact, knowing human nature, they may even give the Christian extra in a way to punish you," the priest said as he dropped money into the other man's hat and walked away.

Uncle Sol turned to his brother sitting next to him and said, "Monty, I love it when the goyim try to teach business to the Copitch brothers."

663. ☆ ☆ ☆ ☆ ☆ ☆ ☆ ☆ ☆ ☆

Melvin came back from the war. His rabbi came to see him the next day to have a heart to heart.

"I know when you are at war it is hard to follow all of the rules of our faith. But now that you are home, it is important that you do."

Melvin thanked the rabbi for his concern and said that he understood. But, that night all he could think about was food, and surprisingly, pork. Over the next few days he found himself obsessing about ham, pork chops, and breakfast pork sausage.

Then Marvin struck on an idea. He would have one last pork meal and then for the rest of his life go back to eating kosher.

Wanting to make his last pork meal amazing he called a Chinese restaurant, way outside of the neighborhood, and ordered Peking Roast Suckling Pig.

The next day, he went to the restaurant and the place was packed. The only table left was in the place of honor, right in the middle of the dining area, reserved for him and his roast pig. Positive he would not be seen by anyone from his synagogue, he sat down.

The chef himself brought out the expensive meal. The suckling pig was presented on a bed of roasted potatoes and a vast assortment of colorful roasted vegetables. The golden skin of the pig glistened, and the bright red apple in the pig's mouth made the presentation picture perfect.

Just then, the rabbi happened by and saw what was going on. He rushed in and said, "Melvin! What are you doing?"

Melvin looked shocked, "Rabbi I ordered a baked apple, look at all the trouble they went too!"

"Ever notice now many lawyers name their daughters Sue?"

664.   ☆ ☆ ☆ ☆ ☆ ☆ ☆ ☆

A man was siting down to watch the bowl games on New Year's Day. He flipped on the TV and nothing but static. He checked the wires and they looked fine, so he went outside to check the satellite dish. There was a huge gorilla swinging from his dish! The man went inside and quickly called the police.

"Sure, sure," the cop said, "a gorilla hanging from your satellite dish. Why don't you sleep it off!" Then the cop hung up on him.

The man was furious, the game was about to start. There was a gorilla on his roof. What was he supposed to do? Then he got an idea, "There can't be that many gorillas around, maybe it escaped from the zoo."

He called the zoo and they were so happy to hear from him. "We have a van out looking for the gorilla, I'll radio our driver and get him right over there.

As soon as the man got out to the front yard, the zoo van screeched to a stop in front of his house. The zoo man assured him that he could capture the gorilla.

"But I will need your help," explained the zoo man.

"Anything, the game has just started," the homeowner yelled.

The zoo man opened the back of the van and released a huge German Shepherd. The dog went nuts running around and barking up at the gorilla, who was happily sitting on the peak of the roof.

The zoo man handed the homeowner a big handgun and then pulled a ladder off the top of the van, leaning it up against the house.

"Now listen carefully," the zoo man yelled over the barking. "I'm going to take this long pole with a nail on the end, up the ladder, and onto your roof. When I'm on the roof, I'm going to poke that gorilla with this big sharp pole until the gorilla falls off the roof. That dog is specially trained to grab the boy parts of that there gorilla. The gorilla will freeze so his parts won't get torn off. That will give me time to get down the ladder and capture him. Got it?"

"Yeah," yelled the homeowner as the zoo man started up the ladder. "But what about this gun?"

"Oh, man... that's the most important part!" yelled the zoo man. "If that there gorilla pushes me off the roof, <u>shoot that fucking dog!</u>"

I have been telling this last joke since I was in high

school and I still find it hilarious.

If you want to see more funnies, please check out my blog:

http://peopletoons.blogspot.com/

Thanks for reading my book, and thank you for encouraging my behavior,

Phil

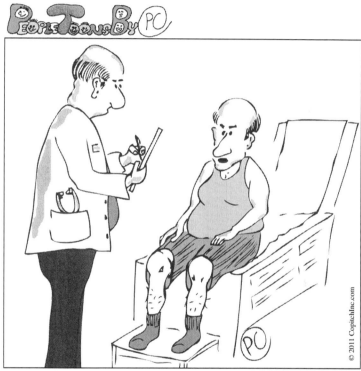

"If 50 is the new 30, how come my knees feel like they're 80?"

8. Encore Cartoons

"Now that I think about it, when I was little I did wonder if Santa hated me."

"According to my blog, your treatment plan earns only three stars."

"I know from your brochure that you graduated... but what was your G.P.A.?"

"I have 49 beautiful wives, Doc. What do you mean I need <u>more</u> exercise?"

Other Books by Dr. Copitch:
See: Amazon.com, Kindle, iPad, or Smashwords.com
- Jokes I Can Read To You: Plus cartoons! (Chapter 1 of this book for kids to read.)
- Basic Parenting 101 The Manual Your Child Should Have Been Born With
- Chutzpah Marketing: Simple Low Cost Secrets to Building Your Business Fortune
- Anatomy For Martial Artists
- Chutzpah Marketing for Mental Health Professionals: The missing manual from your graduate school education
- Phone Scripts For Mental Health Professionals That Fill Your Schedule
- How To Make Money From Your Website or Blog: From basics to money in five hours
- Change: How to bring real change to your life: The psychology and secrets of highly effective people
- Life's Laws For New Adults: Mastering Your Social I.Q

Made in the USA
Lexington, KY
04 April 2014